Breaking Down the Walls

50 COURAGEOUS & SUCCESSFUL YEARS AT THE FOREFRONT OF THE WOMEN'S MOVEMENT

NORMA YAEGER

VESST Investment Partnership LP, d/b/a
VESST Publishing

Breaking Down the Walls:
50 Courageous & Successful Years at the Forefront of the Women's Movement

by Norma Yaeger

Copyright 2012 VESST Publishing
Cover design: Monkey C Media

ISBN 978-0-9857468-1-0

To My Husband – Dr. Lawrence Yaeger –
Thank you for your continuing support during my
successful and difficult times.

To My Children –Victor, Stephen, Sheri, Elysa, & Tod–
I am very proud of you and what you have
become as adults.

To my Grandchildren – Stacey, David, Naomi,
Callie, & Seth –
I adore each and every one of you.

Norma Yaeger under the stock ticker in the Beverly Hills office of Drexel Burnham Lambert

Contents

INTRODUCTION

Michelle Morton
President and CEO, Pacific American Securities
May 2012

Norma was absolutely extraordinary in the financial industry – and still is. I have never met her equivalent. It is hard enough to run counter to a culture that excludes women, as Norma did beginning in 1962. It is even more difficult to run counter to a culture that rewards questionable ethics. Norma maintained her integrity throughout her career and achieved financial success.

To understand how rare she is, you have to understand the financial industry. People are attracted to this industry because they can make a lot of money. A certain kind of personality gravitates to the money. Because there is so much of it available, the industry doesn't pull in the best people, in terms of their values, ethics, and character.

What is character? It's how you behave when no one's looking over your shoulder. In this business, as in all business, there is corruption; temptation is always in front of you. You learn fast that you can "pay to play." For example, when you own a brokerage firm, you can use political connections to increase your business. You can take advantage of influence-peddling. You can contribute to political fundraising campaigns, then make sure that the elected official sets you up with golden opportunities. You can sit on the board of a pension plan and bring them business, and they'll pay you off in trading. Clients frequently make it clear to stockbrokers that they expect something beyond just good service, and brokers frequently comply. Worshipping the dollar and playing by the rules tend to be mutually exclusive.

Norma followed the rules. She had the discipline to regulate herself. She was completely honest regardless of the consequences. She did not allow the system to dictate her behavior. And she was able to build her two brokerage firms and successfully compete against companies with more technology, more seasoned traders, and more products on offer, on a playing field made uneven by backroom deals. People don't realize you can make a profit by doing the right thing. That's such a foreign concept, but it shouldn't be, and Norma's success proves that.

Norma's influence and her basic business values had a profound effect on me. I had worked at BNY Mellon Asset Management on their marketing team, providing investment management services to high net worth individuals. Then I became Interim President of Meyers Capital Management, LLC, working with Shelly Meyers who was quite brilliant. I was helping her and honing my skills at the same time, in anticipation of someday owning my own firm. After I had been there about a year, Shelly introduced me to Norma.

When I worked with Norma to buy her firm and transition Yaeger Capital Markets into Pacific American Securities, I realized that I was a kid. After seventeen years in the business, I still had a lot to learn. I was so lucky to have Norma to learn from. She helped me craft my identity as a professional, placing the fact that I'm a woman and a minority second, so that I would never just be a figurehead for the firm. She modeled for me how to have a clear vision and how to maintain my integrity. She taught me to know my craft and to understand all aspects of the industry.

That was rare, too. Most people in the industry have an area of expertise, but Norma understood the financial, client, and marketing sides of the industry, the complexity of the regulations, and all the different products being offered. She is a Renaissance woman.

I really don't know how she did it. My upbringing had prepared me to aim high and be assertive. My parents believed in possibility. I had a great-aunt, Emily Waters, who was one of the first Black women to be admitted to Julliard. My aunt, Cicely Tyson, was a trailblazer in Hollywood. I was taught that change could and should happen, and that I should be part of it. When I graduated in 1982 from Hood College for Women (a sister school for the U.S. Naval Academy), it was expected that we would either be mothers or have careers – and if you were going to choose motherhood, you had better be engaged by October of your senior year and wedded the following June. However, at least we could choose to have careers if we wanted them.

Norma was raised without that choice, without anyone teaching her that she had that choice. I know that I still face racism and sexism – it's not prevalent but it exists – but Norma had to deal with doors slamming in her face and people not taking her seriously for decades. There weren't organizations for women to help her. She had to take mentoring where she could find it to gain the education she needed.

These days, the financial industry is full of Ivy League graduates and MBAs. Anyone with political connections can open a brokerage firm, and if they know the right people, they'll succeed. Norma had to fight her way up. She persevered, survived difficult times, and worked hard.

And she did it all while raising children who are successful and bright, responsible, contributing members of society. I own and manage a brokerage firm, too, but I just have a dog. I can't believe I know somebody who achieved both a successful career and having a wonderful family. It's amazing to even do one.

Norma is still known; people in the industry still remember who she is, even though she has been retired for over a decade. I think people responded so well to her because she was authentic and uncompromising. She was a little bit of a spitfire, but it was her confidence in herself and her abilities (confidence in a woman is not a bad thing) that attracted clients and colleagues to her. She was also a good marketer and wouldn't take no for an answer. She instilled the highest values in her employees – I think of her as the proverbial iron fist in a velvet glove.

I wish that her influence on the industry could survive and spread. We need more people with her willpower and values. The culture of the industry has changed over the course of my career. The system has always been set up to invent different ways to make money. The nature of investing is innovation – so you get invented products like the bundling and re-selling of mortgages, but the system also invented mutual funds so that people who don't have a lot of money can participate in the market. Like anywhere, people have good ideas and bad ideas. Unfortunately, there haven't been a lot of good ideas lately.

They say power corrupts. Well, so does money. It's not that everyone on Wall Street is corrupt, but priorities have changed. Brokerage firms used to worry about their clients and employees. Now the overriding factor for stockbrokers is getting returns for their investors, and they will do anything for that because they're afraid that if they don't, they'll lose their jobs.

The antidote for fear is courage. Norma had courage – she taught it and she embodied it. She was incredible.

CHAPTER ONE
Fight, Flight, Freeze, or Bond

On Thursday, September 18, 2008, I woke at 4:30 a.m. The hour wasn't unusual for me but the circumstances certainly were.

Three days before, Lehman Brothers had done the unthinkable and declared bankruptcy. Lehman was the fourth largest investment bank in the U.S.A., a twenty-billion-dollar company – that's billion with a "b." That's greater than the gross domestic product of nearly half the world's nations.

Two days before, on September 16, the Federal Reserve threw an 85-million-dollar lifeline to American International Group. AIG insured banks. AIG was supposed to *be* the lifeline and it was drowning.

And all of the largest investment banks were going down with it. Bear Stearns, where I was an Account Executive in the '70s, had already collapsed. Merrill Lynch fed itself to Bank of America at a fire sale price. Goldman Sachs and Morgan Stanley converted to "bank holding companies" so they could receive Federal Reserve funds, but they were still in jeopardy. No one knew how much money they were bleeding out.

These weren't the pillars of the financial world collapsing. They were the ground the financial world stood on and now they were sinkholes. You look at a sinkhole, you wonder, where on earth did all the *earth* go?

I was up early not to work, as usual, but because I couldn't sleep. I was thinking about the people I knew. Banks are made of individuals – my family, my friends, my colleagues. Their families, their lives, their life's work.... What was going to happen to them?

This was a living nightmare.

The stock market opens in New York at 9:30 a.m., 6:30 a.m. in California. I traded from my office on the West Coast for thirty years and I never missed an opening bell.

Though I sold my institutional brokerage firm, Yaeger Capital Markets, in 1998, I was (and still am) a registered representative for the company under its new name: Pacific American Securities, LLC. The success of the company mattered a great deal to me, and there were all my personal investments to manage, too. That Thursday I was already awake when my alarm rang at 4:30 a.m. My feet hit the floor before it finished ringing.

Larry, my husband, would get up soon. He's a surgeon and has kept odd hours for years. We also just like spending our mornings together.

I went to my desk and turned on my computer. While it booted I gazed out the window at the moon, just past full, paling in the sunrise over Encino. Then I refocused on the computer. The first thing I did online was navigate to *The Wall Street Journal* website. Their headline read: "Worst Crisis Since '30s, With No End Yet In Sight."

Well, I said to myself, here comes the avalanche.

I've said that a few times in my life. I've seen many of these crises and they always pass. The market always recovers. From October 6 to 10, 2008, the Dow dropped by 18% and I didn't sell a share of stock.

My friends were calling me, asking what was happening, what should they do? I told them, wait, just wait, do not sell a thing! The avalanche will only take you down if you let it!

I knew this was primal fear they were feeling. I didn't underrate that. The fight-or-flight response is uncontrollable and it dominated those panicking investors for months.

They couldn't fight a market crash. It was a mass crisis of confidence, too intangible. So they fled instead, selling their stocks and driving the market further down.

Some investors had the "freeze" response. They didn't sell their stocks because they were paralyzed with fear, suffering the same feeling of panic as everyone else.

I held on to my stocks for a different reason. I read the situation, compared it to my past experiences, and decided that that was my best choice.

There is also a fourth classic response to danger: bonding. Individuals who feel threatened can band together to pool their resources. That includes wisdom.

I became a broker in 1962. To my knowledge at the time, I was the only woman in the business. (I heard of Muriel Siebert, the first woman to purchase a seat on the New York Stock Exchange, a few years later.) As a stock market veteran and a voice of calm, my job in a crash is to hold the hands of my clients and my friends and share my wisdom. I try to help them understand that they don't have to go under; there is a place to stand where the snow won't take you down. One thing I know, fifty years in the business: even if you think you've hit bottom, don't sell.

How can I be so calm? Well, I rode out my fear a long time ago, and it had nothing to do with the stock market.

* * *

When I sold my brokerage firm in 1998, I was executing several million dollars' worth of trades each day.

Four decades earlier, a mother of two, I didn't even have a say in where I lived. I was thirty years old.

My family moved from Brooklyn to the Catskills in 1960. I was not part of that decision. I had just returned from Florida, where I'd been living with my sons, Victor and Stephen. A doctor had prescribed sunshine and salt water to heal the chronic bronchitis of my younger son, Stephen. Florida did cure him, but when we came home my husband (my first husband, Sam) greeted me with the news that he had changed careers and we were moving upstate.

Sam was a cutter in the garment industry, a dead-end job with no increase in salary possible. Both of us had been unhappy with his direction in life – the only direction I had, too.

Then Sam's friend Ben, an electrician, accepted an offer from a builder to wire a new development of homes up in the Catskills. He brought Sam in as a partner and trained him, but Ben wouldn't be working on the houses himself. Only Sam would be going up there, with his family.

For the sake of our wobbling marriage, I had to believe that Sam's decision and the Catskills would change our lives for the better. He would make money and gain some self-confidence, and I would stop worrying.

* * *

Playing Canasta on a porch in Loch Sheldrake, summer sunshine with just enough of a cool breeze – the first year we lived up in the Catskills wasn't so bad. We even had a few laughs, thanks to the Borscht Belt comedians who busted out their best for the town. Sam's wages weren't what we expected but we managed, until a pot of water on my stove boiled over into a pan of frying potatoes – and hot oil – and our kitchen went up in flames. (I always was better at baking.) Thankfully the owner of the building had insurance, but we had to leave.

On such slim notice options were limited, so we rented one of the builder's unsold houses in the development where Sam had been working. Spending spring and summer in a new house out on Lake Louise Marie – doesn't that sound lovely?

Sure, until the day Sam's pay didn't come. All of a sudden the builder wasn't available to explain that missing check. (Funny how he was always around when he had something to say.)

Weeks passed, still no pay. My husband was begging money from our families. I gave birth to my daughter in August and that same month, the builder stood on our lawn and yelled, "You got to pay your rent or I'll throw you and your family out!"

My husband yelled back, "What about you? When are you going to pay me? For all this work I've done!"

"Well, I'm bankrupt so you better figure out something else!"

The Catskills had certainly changed our lives.

We had no income. With the summer over there were no jobs. So in September of 1961 my husband went to live with his mother in Brooklyn. When he found work in the city, we would be able to join him. Until then, we made a deal with the bankrupt builder: I would stay with the children in the house on the lake until spring. Then, out.

Did you hear the joke about the Catskills in the winter? No? That's because there aren't any.

Oh, there's plenty of winter. Wind that rolls down from the mountains and rattles the walls, iced phone lines, closed eyes and frozen eyelashes as you struggle from your front door to the curb, reminds you why the two hundred dollars (in 1961 – $1,400 today) you wanted to put into IBM stocks, you spent winterizing your car instead. Life is about prioritizing, when you have enough to prioritize, but I'm coming to that....

Plenty of winter, no jokes, because all the comedians left in September. They packed their little notebooks, the lawn games, the dance bands, the hotel managers and the hotel managers' wives and the hotel managers' employees and the hotel managers' employees' families, too, they packed all the vacation in the vacation towns and flew south with it. Nobody stays in the Catskills, are you crazy? Listen, Rip Van Winkle goes up in the Catskills alone one fall, it takes twenty years off his life.

Well here I was, alone with three children.

September, all right. It was still hot and I had a car. I could drive into town, go to temple, visit the few people still left, play a little more Canasta. It was almost like the previous September, when we were living in town.

It wasn't quiet yet at the lake, either. The geese were still blatting overhead. The smaller birds still chirruped through the mornings. And my sons, ages 6 and 7, trumpeted news and ideas and games when they came home from school.

October, Chico Marx died. One more comedian gone. October, I was still taking walks, holding Elysa in my arms,

11

Victor and Stephen and our dog Butch running all over. We looked at that big sky over the lake and all right, so the colors of the trees were beautiful. But we were always coming back to those big, empty houses in the development, staring at us as we passed.

Of course windows are eyes. Anything is eyes if you need someone to see you. Would you rather be paranoid or lonely?

Then I saw a bear across the lake, and he saw me. There had been reports for weeks about bears attacking people. I ran the children inside and closed the curtains and the blinds so he shouldn't see people. I had to make my house look like the other houses, locked up, but Butch was a yapper. I shut him in the bathroom and hoped the house was built well enough to muffle him. We didn't walk much after that.

I'm angry now, for myself back then. I don't run away. I don't hide, no matter what's coming at me. But back then, I had to play dead.

November, the trees lost their leaves. I was reliving the nightmares I'd had when I was pregnant with Elysa and veering between deep depression and acute anxiety. Once I had panicked so much – afraid that when I went into labor Sam would be working and wouldn't get there in time, afraid I wouldn't make it to the hospital, forty-five minutes away – anyway, the doctor had given me a Librium, and I couldn't get up for two days. Some lucid moments but mostly asleep – for two whole days.

I came to, I was okay. But for the rest of the pregnancy I had had nightmares, waking up in a deep sweat. They were always about being alone. I had this terrible, terrible fear of being alone and now, by the lake, I was.

December, the snow started.

NORMA YAEGER

I was born and raised in Brooklyn where the snow is very pretty for an hour, maybe half a day, until the snowplows shove it into black and gray piles and we all stop looking at it and get back to our lives.

The first time it snowed, it was lovely. I think there was a moon over the lake that night; I remember that "Moon River" was all over the radio at the time.

The next time it snowed, okay, very nice, like when you're at a friend's and their children are performing and you're thinking, okay, very nice, how much more?

The snowstorm that dropped ten feet on the lake and the school bus couldn't get through to pick up the boys and the four panes of glass in the front door were covered and some of the windows were covered too – I could have lived without.

The snowstorm when the electricity and the heat went out and the electric company wasn't going to turn it back on because we hadn't paid them, so I had to threaten them with liability if we died of exposure – not so good.

The snowstorm when Elysa had a 104° fever and the police had to deliver her medicine to us on a snowplow – that was bad. One snowstorm after another after another, I couldn't drive, I couldn't get anywhere, I thought I was going to lose Butch in a drift, even the boys had had enough snow....

It was getting harder and harder for me to wake up in the morning. I would lie in bed and wonder how I was going to stretch the food that day, that's how bad the news was from Brooklyn. I tried to have one egg a day and give the rest of the eggs to the boys. If the weather was all right and the school bus could get through, they could have breakfast and lunch at school. Dinner, sometimes okay – but sometimes I was thinning out the milk and adding white bread to the chopped meat to stretch it.

13

You think maybe you'll feel a sense of accomplishment when you figure out how to survive a shortage of food. I didn't. I just felt mean, watering down powdered milk that was watered down in the first place, one of the days they couldn't deliver the fresh milk.

I wanted not just to be angry, but to have the energy to be angry. To blame someone else, the builder or my husband; but the blame game won't boost you out of bed when you're depressed.

I tell you who I was getting up in the morning for – Jack LaLanne and his exercise show on television. "Trimnastics"! That way at least I was moving. He was so buoyant, he had that big grin that hardly fit on his head, but he made you earn it. He'd work up to it for half the show and just when you had had it and couldn't do any more, he brought out that smile. Besides, you can't sit back into your depression when a man who looks like a comic book superhero is raising his eyebrows at you.

There was Captain Kangaroo, too. Sometimes I turned on his show even when the boys weren't home, just for a familiar face.

But I craved news. News! The television news shows were so short. We only got the local newspaper, and then only on the days the truck could deliver – listen, that was not a year not to have access to the news. The Bay of Pigs happened in April. Freedom Riders were being attacked and in the summer Alabama declared martial law because of race riots. President Kennedy said in public address, Americans, build fallout shelters! You understand, he told us *we needed to be building fallout shelters.* There was a wall going up in Berlin and the Soviets had started nuclear testing again. If the world was going to end in nuclear war, I at least wanted to know about it!

And I was a New Yorker, born and bred. New York City, you always feel the great things happening. You may not be in the offices where the great events are being planned and decided, but you know they're happening. I had studied business in college and I knew, it wasn't just a matter of money changing hands. It was the great force of Change, happening all the time. New York was the biggest train in the world and I was missing it.

I was doing laundry. Two boys, a baby – I was doing a lot of laundry. I hated my children's clothes. I hated my clothes.

And I was making slipcovers for the furniture that came with the house, because the boys jumped on it. Too bad they never broke any of it, I hated that ugly furniture.

And I was baking. Poor Jack LaLanne, so good about health, encouraging me to eat nutritional food and avoid empty calories. Cookies, cake, whatever I could think of and had the ingredients for, down it went. The boys would come in saying, "Mmmm, Mommy, what'd you make that smells so good!" Tracking snow all over the kitchen floor but what did I have but time to clean it up?

When they came home we did schoolwork together, puzzles, played games. We spread sheets over chairs and played Going Hunting in our tent. I am five feet tall and what with watering down my brain as well as the milk, I felt as much a child as they were, watching the westerns on TV, reading Dr. Seuss.

Until I went to bed and then I was old, old, old. Bad if the lake was quiet. Worse if the wind was blowing. Even worse if I could hear snow tick against the window, just when I was about to fall asleep.

I wasn't sure which was more terrible, feeling like the snow was a personal attack – especially when the TV, my only connection to the outside world, went out –

Eichmann, put to death in Israel for his crimes, the TV went out right in the middle of the news report – or knowing that there was nothing personal about it. My family and I didn't matter a bit to the snow or the bears or the big, empty houses all around us.

I could have called someone, but who? My friends in town had their own troubles, their own snowdrifts to shovel out, and Canasta friends are... Canasta friends. My sister Mildred in New Jersey, my best friend, but she knew how tough it was for me. How many times can you call with the same problems, no solutions? Things weren't so lucrative for her either.

My Uncle Abe and Aunt Lois visited once and they helped me. In those times the person that gives, gives from the heart, and I don't know what I would have done without them. (A year full of many changes later, I was able to pay them back.)

I could have called my husband... no.

I could have gone to sleep with the radio, I guess, but what was I going to hear, six million songs about the Twist for people dancing in the city. Or Nat King Cole, I liked him very much, but he was singing all about "Let There Be Love" along with the rest of those people with plenty of people to love them. Or Patsy Cline falling to pieces. Or Roy Orbison crying. Maybe better off with silence.

* * *

One day Butch dragged home the carcass of some dead wild animal and started eating it.

Well, that's how you get rabies. I called Frank Pappora at the Dodge Inn a few miles away – his family was so helpful, they always called to see if I needed anything when they drove into town – anyway, he came with his truck and took away the carcass. He took Butch, too, to the pound.

That night lying in bed, I wondered if it was so silent because the boys had stopped crying? Or because they were crying into their pillows so I wouldn't hear? They were so angry at me, especially Stephen, that dog was his pal. "You're a terrible mom! If Captain Kangaroo was here, he'd hate you! You go away and don't come back, Mom!"

It was so quiet.

My children hated me. I hated their clothes.

I began to have the same thoughts I'd been having for weeks, maybe months. All this could go away.

Of course you always think about methods – sleeping pills – and all this could go away. Even if I didn't have the pills, even if there was a snowstorm, the police could deliver some on a snowplow like they did for Elysa's 104° fever. I just say she has another one and, oh, when you bring her medicine, also the doctor will give you sleeping pills to bring out, too. So easy.

"Bottom" is when that plan feels rational. "Bottom" is when you think, I was crazy to have children. "Bottom" is when the only way to solve your situation is to subtract yourself and your babies from it. "Bottom" is the bottom line showing you, a human being, to be the greatest loss of your life.

I don't remember if I got up for Jack LaLanne the next day or for the children or just because my body was still there and it had needs separate from mine. I rushed the boys out of the house to school, and wondered if Elysa was sick again, she was so fussy that morning. Still in my night-gown, I stepped outside to get the milk. I heard the front door close. I turned around and it was locked.

Every other way into the house was locked, too, because of the bears.

The baby was crying. I was in my slippers and nightgown, panicking. The door was locked, the phone inside. Nothing but snow everywhere. Nothing! *Nothing!* Was I screaming out loud or was that in my head? What was I going to do? I was alone!

I was *alone.*

This was my greatest fear and it was happening to me, right here, right now.

The baby was crying. My hands were shaking with panic.

Really, I had nothing but milk and snow.

Then... I didn't know what I was doing until I was doing it. I took off a slipper, put my fist in it, and punched at one of the glass panes in the door. I don't know how many times it took, but I hit the glass until it broke and I could reach inside, push the button, and unlock the door.

At that moment I knew, I am a woman who will punch through glass if I need to.

But I didn't know that I knew that.

The rest of that day was like all the others, except I taped cardboard over the broken glass to keep the wind out. I did the same baking, played the same games with the boys when they came home, had the same thoughts about sleeping pills at night. Nothing had changed that I knew about.

* * *

Things got worse. And worse. You think, this is it, it can't get worse than this! And what happens? "Bottom" is just a cliff ledge on the way down.

A few weeks later I decided to see an analyst. I needed somebody to tell me something good. I needed him to hold my hand and tell me that everything was going to be okay.

Well the analyst had just lost a child so he wasn't really the best person for me to talk to.

Later, much later, when I was learning the ups and downs of the stock market, I realized there *is* no such thing as "bottom." If the market falls far enough, you assume you've hit bottom; but it's just a convenient phrase. Nobody ever knows for sure.

Spring came to Lake Louise Marie, and spring is supposed to be about hope and rebirth. But spring can be ugly. That awful yellow green on some of the trees, the rest of them still bare and black and skinny. The mud, the raw wind. You think you've finally seen the last snowstorm and another one happens. And the builder comes back and says, "That's it! I have to sell the houses now! Get out and take your slipcovers with you!"

Where am I going to go, three children, the clothes on our backs?

To my mother-in-law's house, while I looked for an apartment.

All those mother-in-law jokes, they come from somewhere.

Life isn't neat. It doesn't turn around all in a minute, and you don't always know when you've learned something.

I did learn. I knew what I could do when I had to. I knew, no matter how far down you fall, you don't sell.

But I didn't have words for those things I knew – yet.

Then and Now

Poverty doesn't look the same now as it did then, at first glance. Back then, poverty was watching your children get thinner as you tried to stretch the little food you had. Today, you can find cheap food – eventually it will make you sick, but it's food.

Homelessness, though – that hasn't changed. There were over four million foreclosures on homes in the United States from 2007 to 2011.[1] Where did all those people go? Did they all have relatives who would open their homes to them and their families?

I was terrified in the Catskills. I had been brought up in a comfortable home with no financial problems, and being that poor, with three children to take care of, was a real eye-opener. My parents needed financial help themselves at that time, so I couldn't lean on them. I was really panicking before my Uncle Abe and Aunt Lois gave me a loan.

With all my fear in those days, I did have the feeling that if worse came to worst, I could rely on the government to help. It would provide a cushion, thank god. I think of that a great deal today, how much I needed to know that the government would be there if no one else was. Many years later, my parents had real need of the government. They had had financial reversals and ended up depending on Social Security. They also never had health insurance – people of that generation frequently didn't – so without Medicare and Medicaid, my mother would not have received healthcare.

---

1 Christie, Les. Foreclosures fall to lowest level since 2007. *CNNMoney*. Jan. 12, 2012. http://money.cnn.com/2012/01/12/real_estate/foreclosures/index.htm. Accessed May 24, 2012.

Political attacks on government programs aiding the poor occur regularly. We are in another cycle of that right now, as members of Congress clamor to stop assistance such as the food stamp program in the name of decreasing the national debt. But poverty is truly a trap. You cannot get out of it without some kind of hand up, and not everyone has an Uncle Abe and Aunt Lois.

I don't care if there are people who abuse the government assistance programs like food stamps, unemployment insurance, and welfare. Those programs allow the people who need help to have it. Abuses happen in every system. The government can find ways to identify abusers of the system, but it must not punish the truly needy by ending the programs. I will never forget begging the electric company to keep our heat on during that long winter. When you look down and realize that you yourself need a safety net, you don't want to take that away from anyone, ever again.

CHAPTER TWO
Always Keep Moving

"NORMA? IS EVERYTHING all right?"

Sam's mother knocked on the bathroom door.

"Norma?"

"Yeah, yeah! One more page!" I called back.

The bathroom was my favorite place to read, and still is. Usually I read books but that day in 1962 it was an article about Margot Fonteyn and Rudolf Nureyev. They had danced together for the first time in February at the Royal Ballet. Up in the Catskills, I'd missed the sensation. A few key newspapers weren't delivered because of snow.

I had always wanted to be a dancer. I took ballet and tap classes from age eight to college. I attended public performances whenever I could. At James Madison High School in Brooklyn I joined the Twirler Team. At the City College of New York, I argued the college band manager into casting a Drum Majorette instead of a Drum Major. They'd never had a girl lead the band before. It helped that I was five feet tall with long, lustrous black hair; who wouldn't want me out in front? I froze my knickers off for that gig, trekking up to Lewiston Stadium in my short skirt and white boots, my big C sweater.

I also won a scholarship for dance at Carnegie Hall. Every day I walked from college at 23rd and Lex to Carnegie Hall at 57th and 7th. (Free exercise!) There I took ballet, a Martha Graham class, and flamenco. I especially loved clacking the castanets, like choice words in an argument. But the secret to flamenco is not its wild spirit. You have to have your feet on the ground. The rhythm of your heels – so precise, so complex – makes the dance and the passion possible.

"Norma? Norma, aren't you done yet?" Esther knocked on the bathroom door again. "Norma?"

"In a minute!"

I stopped dancing when I stopped college. Then I had kids. I was almost 32 now, sitting on the toilet, reading about Margot Fonteyn. Everyone expected her to retire. Maybe she expected it, too. Then Nureyev's electric shock to her career made retirement unthinkable. I thought *I* was old; here was Margot, age 42, beginning a whole new life.

What had happened to me? What had happened to my dreams?

"Norma!" Knock knock knock knock!

"All right all right all right all right!"

Sam's mother owned both apartments in a two-apartment house, so Sam and the kids and I moved into the lower one. That didn't mean there was privacy. Esther wasn't a bad person; she just had to be involved in everything at all times. I couldn't accept that. We clashed constantly.

The bathroom was one refuge. My other refuge was staying up late after everyone else was asleep. Midnight was my thinking time. Mostly I thought about money. Should I go into business? What kind of business could I do? I had a

23

license to sell insurance and mutual funds that I'd acquired in the Catskills – but I hadn't been very successful at that. What else, what else....

I still do that, even in my retirement. I look around a street, a neighborhood, a city, and wonder what kind of business does this place need and can I provide it.

Back then, though, I had no optimism. I only worried myself back into paralysis and went to bed.

Every day I woke up to silence: Sam's depression, my fearful brooding. If we spoke, we spatted. Otherwise we said nothing. Now I know, when you stop communicating, your marriage is doomed.

* * *

Living with Esther, I lasted about two months. Then Sam and I moved to Howard Beach, thanks to Sam's new job – as a cutter again – and the remainder of the loan from Aunt Lois and Uncle Abe. We had a nice house, a nice neighborhood, nice families all around us; none of it helped. Sam wasn't so silent anymore. Now he was cutting and critical of me. He blamed me for pushing too hard. He was doing the best he could, why wasn't I more supportive? The Catskills was my fault. Everything was my fault. Eventually he reached the level of verbal abuse.

I started spending a lot of time in the bathroom again.

I hated nagging him, I really did. But I was trying to get through to him. Why couldn't he imagine something better than being a cutter? He couldn't think his way out of who he was. Look at Larry, our neighbor across the street. He had returned from being an Army doctor in Germany and went into private practice. His family was living in Howard Beach temporarily while he worked with an architect to build a beautiful house in Queens. Why couldn't Sam go to school, get a degree, it didn't have to be a medical degree, just anything....

I sounded so shrill to myself. I couldn't think my way out of who I was, either. I didn't even know who I was.

But down deep, I still had the will to move, to take the next step, any step at all. (Always keep moving, no matter what.) Sam told me it was a waste of money but I started therapy again. This time I found a therapist who wasn't grief-stricken and depressed.

Doc Grossman's office was in a lovely townhouse around the corner from Herald Square. His warm office was full of leather furniture in a chestnut brown. My first afternoon there, I cried for an hour.

Somehow Doc deciphered a picture of my life with Sam. Eventually I tried to pull myself together and offer some useful analysis (my husband's name is Samuel, my father's name is Samuel). Doc stopped me.

"Norma, you don't need to go through your family history. You need help *now*. I'm not going to give you psychotherapy. You need to come out of your depression, help your family, help yourself, pick up your boots and *move yourself.* I am going to help you do that."

I cried on the train home, too.

We did end up going over my family history, for months. (I think I was buying time for my poor brain to grasp what Doc was saying.)

I started with my parents, Samuel and Regina Hason. Now there was a marriage built on a deliberate lack of communication. Most of them were back then. (I think some of them still are.) After all, when one person always gives in

25

to the other, that does produce a kind of peace. Both of my parents were Sephardic Jews, and there is no question in a Middle Eastern household in pre-war Brooklyn about who is going to get his way.

Which is probably why the first time I formed a question, I was outside my home. I was six or seven years old when Nona Vieja (Ladino for "old grandmother") took me to temple. The men and women were seated separately. I didn't like that. In fact, I didn't bother questioning the tradition. I skipped straight to resenting it.

How does a child know that something is wrong when it's been done that way for centuries? How does change first spark? I didn't have anyone around me whispering that things should be different. I seemed to know on my own.

Although... I had already had Kindergarten with Mrs. Roundtree by then. Mrs. Roundtree read us a chapter of the Mary Poppins books every day. I loved those books; and Mary Poppins would never have put up with segregated seating. That may sound ridiculous, but such a thought can have enormous impact for a child.

I did not seethe silently. I complained about the separate seating to Nona Vieja on our way home. That was the first of many times someone told me, "You're just like your father."

I took it as the highest compliment.

My father, Nona's grandson, was an atheist. He didn't bother debating with his family about it. He just didn't practice and didn't believe. I'm not sure when the break came; maybe when he was in the Marines for four years. He had hoped to be a doctor but never had the opportunity. After the Marines he applied his considerable intelligence to founding a garment manufacturing company with his brother Nathan. They made plus-sized ladies' dresses and, during WWII, women's uniforms. The company grew until my father was managing a factory with many women at the sewing machines.

I adored him – how smart he was, and savvy, too. He wasn't a people person and preferred animals; he had a coop of racing pigeons (and would later own racehorses). Yet he seemed to work so well with people, and he commanded success in everything he did.

With my mother he succeeded at having a perfectly peaceful marriage – the traditional way. For instance, my mother still practiced Judaism. My father could have ordered her not to keep kosher and she could have fought him on it. Instead, he purposely mixed up all her kosher dishes and towels with the regular ones until she stopped trying. My mother kept the peace the only way she knew how: giving in. (She always bought kosher food, though. He couldn't do anything about that.)

It's easy to look back now and talk about men and women playing traditional roles. "Playing" doesn't convey the depth of that lopsided culture. Men and women *embodied* those roles. I remember watching my parents play cards with their friends. The women wouldn't excuse themselves to go to the bathroom. The men would get up and say, "I have to go to the bathroom." The women would wait until there was a break in the game for coffee, then sneak away to the toilet. The word "bathroom" was not "nice." Anything to do with the female body was taboo.

It was clear to me that women were going to have to fight to get anywhere. My mother gave into my father on everything. Though he expected and accepted it, he didn't respect it. Well, I respected my father and I wanted to be worthy of his respect. Which meant I couldn't be like her; I had to be like him.

And that's what everyone said: You're just like your father.

And oh, how I fought with him.

If he said black, I said white. If he said anything at all, I said the opposite. He'd come home late in the evening and I'd be ready to pick a fight. He was old-fashioned even for that time so topics were easy to come by. I wasn't allowed to go on sleepovers because "girls belong at home"; well he could enforce that, but I could fight it. He'd put down women and I'd put down his opinion. He'd say things like "college makes girls too smart and spoils their chances to get a husband," yet I spent all my time proving to him how smart I was.

I enjoyed the arguments not just because I was getting his attention, but because it felt like exercise. Clashing with him was a pleasure. It was my hobby. And though my younger brothers were treated like kings as was usual for Middle Eastern families, I was my father's favorite. Maybe he liked seeing himself in me. Maybe when he rejected his faith, when he messed up my mother's dishes, he'd been hoping for a little savory opposition.

I went to City College School of Business because math had always been my best subject (and because I won the college fight against my father). Then in sophomore year my best friend Irma and I decided to go to the University of Wisconsin for a summer program in economics.

"Wisconsin?" my father said. "Women sleep home with their parents until they're married. They don't go wandering all over the place. Wisconsin, forget it!"

I was eighteen. That was one argument he was not going to win. And when my father wasn't around my mother said, "If you can pay for it, go, go..."

I was already dating Sam then. He lived one street away from us in Sheepshead Bay. My father had trained him as a cutter so he could help support his family. I had been baby-sitting and working at a neighborhood department store, saving for Wisconsin. Sam offered to help – he was so kind. (Handsome, too.) So I gave him my savings and asked him to send it to me in Wisconsin on a regular basis so I could live on a budget.

Voluntary responsibility! Imagine that! Such was the kind of person who could go to work on Wall Street *and* succeed there... once upon a time.

So Irma and I escaped for a whole summer of economics, tennis, dancing, dating, everything that wasn't my parents, and my hobby, debating. I didn't stop that just because my father wasn't around. I debated with Irma. Her father was a presser at a clothing company and a union member. My father was a manufacturer and non-union. The unions tried to recruit him; they brought in thugs with bats and my father and grandfather were both hurt – but not recruited. So Irma and I argued about the value of unions and not forcing people into things.

(Still true, but I'm on Irma's side of the argument now. People do need the power of numbers. They need to work together to make things right. Just do it with reason, not with force. It sounds so obvious but people forget the obvious.)

I guess I expected a big fight from my father when I came home, especially because I stopped in Chicago for a few days instead of coming straight back to New York.

What I got was silence. He didn't talk to me for a year. He'd say "pass the salt," sure, but he wouldn't argue with me anymore. Our special, fiery friendship was over.

When my father stopped speaking to me, I couldn't ask him for college tuition. So I quit college, and my dance classes.

29

A&S Department Stores hired me as a salesperson in a bridal department. I rose to buyer's assistant, then to purchaser of all the veils for the stores. I ran a division and liked it and was successful at it.

Still my father was silent towards me. So I decided to marry Sam. That opened his mouth.

"Norma, he's not good for you. You're too smart for him. You have it all over him and he'll never be more than a cutter...."

I married Sam in March of 1951. We planned a cruise to Bermuda for our honeymoon. When my A&S manager heard that, she exploded. "Take a week off when we have to sell to the June brides?! No!"

I was in the habit of contradicting, though. I quit that job and went on the cruise with Sam and was seasick the whole time. (Take *that*, Dad.)

When we returned I found a job with Resident Buyers. They bought clothing for department stores in the Midwest who couldn't come to New York to shop it. I was an assistant buyer in the coats and suits department. It was wonderful.... You had to understand people. You had to figure out what they wanted and what they didn't know they wanted. Resident Buyers reminded me that I liked people. I always had; that was one big difference between my father and myself.

My father had retired by now, and had purchased a chicken farm in Lakewood, New Jersey. He had always liked animals, so he cleaned chicken-s**t. Go figure.

After Resident Buyers my next job was to have babies. That took some time to occur. My father's chickens were far more successful than I was; they were prodigious. Sam and I would drive to the chicken farm on the weekends and come home with a car full of eggs.

I did some thinking. I looked around my neighborhood, I wondered....

And I rented a storefront on Ocean Avenue, hand-lettered some signs and flyers, and opened an egg shop. The retail work was fine, a little boring, but the store did well. The bulk of the work, though, was candling the eggs. I held every egg over a candle in a dark room and peered through its shell, making sure it wasn't full of blood or bacteria or a developing chicken (ugh, spooky). It was tedious, mindless work and the repetition started to get to me. I was looking into thousands of glowing gold crystal balls and none of the futures were worth having....

Sam and I conceived in 1953. I closed my egg shop; I didn't miss the candling. The diaper years commenced. Victor was born first, Stephen fifteen months later.

Sometimes when the boys were still in their baby carriage, instead of taking them to the park I wheeled them to a stock brokerage office on the main street of our neighborhood. It was my one pure pleasure of the day. I stood outside the big windows and watched the Dow stock ticker on the wall. I followed a few stocks that looked interesting – American Telephone, General Electric, General Motors – and popped inside to pick up the brokerage's reports on them. Then I read them outside, imagining what I'd buy and how much and when –

"Yes, what about that?" Doc Grossman interrupted.

"What about what?" I said.

"The stock market."

"What do you mean?"

"You say life with Sam in Howard Beach is getting worse."

"It is, he keeps –"

"No. You must change the situation. You are your

31

own solution. No one's going to do this for you. Not your husband, not your father, nobody. *You need to do for you.*"

"Do what, though?"

"Start divorce proceedings. You and Sam are destroying yourselves with each other."

He had said that many times, but divorce was unthinkable. The ugly fiscal realities it would bring....

"Yes," Doc said. "What can you do to face those realities?"

Well, my father couldn't help me. All of his chickens had caught a disease and were put down. He lost the farm. Then he lost most of the rest of his money raising racehorses. I had never seen him fail before.

"Not your father, Norma," Doc said. "You."

"There's nobody else I can ask –"

"Norma, *you*. How can *you* face the fiscal realities? Do you want more loans?"

"No," I said, surprising myself. "No, I don't. Loans aren't a solution. They compound the problem. Literally, with interest."

"So OK," Doc said. "We are talking a salary then. What do you have to offer the world?"

"Not a college education," I said.

"You love the stock market. What about that?"

"You mean selling mutual funds?" I still had the license from New York Life that I'd acquired in the Catskills. "But I wasn't any good at it. I'm not good at much –"

"Norma –" Doc warned.

OK. I couldn't indulge in depression. I had to do for me. But –

"Doc, you know what my prospective clients up in Loch Sheldrake said?" I asked. "They said, 'A *lady*, selling mutual funds? *Ha!!*' They laughed at me."

"And did you listen?" said Doc. "Where is the girl who was just like her father?"

* * *

Therapists invented the term "delayed gratification." They plant an idea in a person's head and it doesn't pay off for months or years....

I'd been in therapy for half a year when I went to Eastern Parkway to visit my old Wisconsin ally, Irma, and her husband, Earl. Earl was making a very nice living at Hornblower & Weeks, a brokerage firm in Manhattan.

I must have been nattering on about stocks; the Dow had been volatile that year and I'd been following it in the papers. *Life* magazine had done a cover story about it in June. The article title was "What went wrong in the wild stock market?" The Dow had also plummeted along with everything else during the Cuban Missile Crisis. It bounced right back, though, when the Russians announced they were pulling their nukes. All the brokerage firms were happily planning for a future.

"You know, Norma," Earl said. "We are starting a training program for stockbrokers at Hornblower & Weeks. We don't have women in this business yet, but we are considering them. Why don't you call my manager for an appointment and see if you can interview for the program?"

"Oh my god, Earl," I said. "*I would love to.* Thank you, thank you!"

Then and Now

I kept the fact that I was seeing a therapist very quiet back then. I was consulting a psychologist, someone who helps people put their lives back together, not a psychiatrist, who handles the very sick. In the 1960s, people didn't differentiate between them. Anyone who knew I was going to a psychologist would have thought I was nuts. Even I wondered to myself, am I crazy?

That has certainly changed over the last fifty years. Now I think we have a new problem: people relying too much on medications to fix their problems, instead of listening to the insights that a psychologist or psychiatrist can bring. My one experience with that kind of medication – Librium – was enough for me. After that knocked me out for two days, I never took another pill like that again. My mental health was too important.

Doc Grossman's approach to mental health was honesty – sometimes painful honesty. "Let's look at your problems," he said. "What's holding you back? What's handcuffing you to your current life?" Of course, we realized that part of the problem was how I'd been raised. For instance, my father's idea of a compliment was, "You're a good driver, you drive just like a man." Women were kept down systematically and thoroughly.

But the most important question Doc asked was, "What are you doing to yourself that's destructive?" No matter how you are raised, there are choices that you and only you make that continue your problems. If you make different choices, you start to change. Doc urged me to pull myself out of the past and fight for a new life. That took a lot of support, which I wouldn't have had if I didn't listen to Doc's outside perspective. It took enormous courage, which is hard to muster if you have dulled your senses with prescriptions. And it took strength to accept that I had no excuses to fall back on; I was responsible for pursuing my own happiness.

CHAPTER THREE
Selling Intangibles

I NEED THIS JOB.

The A train clacked toward Manhattan. It was spring, 1962, one year after I crept away from the Catskills to move in with my mother-in-law.

Though it was a weekday, the train was running at Sunday speed, definitely not fast enough. Every time it unnecessarily slowed for a turn I thought again – I need this job.

Life was worse after Earl offered me a possible way out. You'd think that would be the time for hope and optimism to rush in and brighten my outlook, but no. Earl had opened a little window in my cinder-block cell. In this new light, the cell looked terrifying.

It was a three-month wait before I could take the Hornblower & Weeks test for admission into their training program, so I had plenty of time to assess that cell. Bills. Future bills. College for three children. A cutter's salary. The five-thousand-dollar loan from Aunt Lois and Uncle Abe – in today's dollars, $35,000 – and not much of it left.

I didn't treat money like an allowance anymore, cash in hand. I understood the concept of investment, that sometimes going into debt is necessary for growth. But that $5,000 – what was that invested in?

Sam.

Sam was supposed to grow enough to pay that back. Plus he had to provide an income that would never force us to borrow like that again. Could he even keep up with inflation, let alone grow?

"He's never going to cut it," I said to Doc Grossman one week. "Is he?"

Doc had said enough. He didn't need to say any more. Sam was going to be a cutter for life.

That's when my depression flipped into desperation. I needed this job.

Understand, I didn't want this to be true. I wanted to believe in my husband. I stayed in the Catskills that winter because I felt guilty. I felt disloyal toward him and that is a wretched feeling.

But if you have kids, you look reality in the face or reality will kick you in the butt.

I had one other thought on the train: "Test! What kind of test? A school test? I've been a homemaker for ten years! How am I going to do this?"

The train took another slow turn. *I needed this job.*

* * *

The company psychologist placed a booklet on the desk and folded his hands on it before he looked at me.

"There is no right or wrong on this test," he stated.

OK, so this wasn't school.

I was still anxious. My throat had closed up. I felt like I was swallowing sharpened pencils.

What did he mean, no right or wrong? Was there a crazy or not crazy on this test? I studied his face but there was no emotion there, no clues. He was absolutely neutral, crisp and clean as the filing cabinets around the walls. It's fashionable these days to look back at office culture of the 1960s – the lines of the furniture, the cuts of the suits – and label it either "cool" or oppressive. Straight lines, blocks of color, no excessive frills – it didn't strike me as rigid and controlling. Away from the ragged edges of children's arguments and a husband's excuses and putting a house back together after a day's use of it, this crispness was a relief. I was in a world of grown-ups. I didn't need the psychologist to be warm and relatable. I needed this job.

The psychologist explained that this was a three-day test. (Thanks to Lois and Abe, I had hired babysitters with the last of the loan.) The first two days I would be completing written tests; the third day he would interview me in his capacity as a psychologist. By the third day, I was sure, my throat would be so closed up I wouldn't be able to talk.

He left me alone with the booklet and dark pencils. Actually, I'm sure I wasn't alone, but I can't remember any other applicants. I was so focused my peripheral vision had shut down. There was only the test.

The first day involved about four hours of personality questions. I've never taken an official IQ test but I'd be shocked if that weren't included. IQ tests were considered nearly infallible at the time, and this kind of testing company was hired by all the brokerages to be on the cutting edge of psychological profiling.

Many of the questions gauged career interest and aptitude. "If you were building a house, would you be the architect, the contractor, or the electrician?" Well it depends. Is the house in the Catskills? Am I getting paid or is the realtor broke? (Of course I didn't write that.)

Then there were the questions I didn't know how to classify, and still don't. "Would you kiss a man? Would you kiss a woman? Would you kiss children?" I took a long pause over that one. What on earth were they asking here? Was the psychologist being honest when he said there was no right or wrong on this test? What kind of kiss? Were they trying to figure out whether I was a lesbian, a nymphomaniac, a pedophile?

This was the real IQ test. Do I answer the way I want to, or the way I think they want me to? Do they want to know who I am, or do they want to know that I am who they want me to be? *I need this job....*

This was also the real test of mental health. Because if you slide down the slope of trying to second-guess and out-think and out-maneuver – that way madness lies.

I answered the way I would naturally. Yes, I'd kiss all three, why not? I'd kiss my mother, I'd kiss my aunt, kissing is a friendly thing to do. I answered all the questions that way, just as I am.

I was exhausted that evening but I didn't short-change my home-life. I didn't talk much, especially to Sam, but the children were fed and in bed, the dishes were done, the house was clean. He couldn't say I hadn't done "my job." I didn't give him any room to pick a fight; I couldn't afford to get stirred up, in case I angrily let slip my secret. Nobody knew I was taking this test but Earl and Irma, so I just needed to keep everything very calm and quiet.

Why keep a secret at all? Because I knew him. I didn't see the point in creating a problem before the problem really existed. That's just good sense. If Hornblower accepted me, that would be time enough.

* * *

The second day of tests was all about sales. Most of them were either/or scenarios. For example: "You're trying to sell shares of an airline's stock to a prospective client. Which of the following do you do first? (a) Tell the client that you like this airline stock, (b) Tell the client he should like this airline stock, (c) Describe the airline company in detail, or (d) Ask the client about his current stock holdings."

The psychologist had stated again that there was no right or wrong here, but I wasn't treading water so much today. I could feel these questions; I had something to come back at them with.

Back in the Catskills, after Sam's checks had stopped coming, I'd had the idea of selling life insurance. There was a New York Life office in town. I took their test for a license and a license to sell shares in mutual funds, too. I got a little training and began to approach people in my temple and around the neighborhood. Cut your teeth on the people you know, then spread out from there, it's just networking.... Well, it turned out that's the hardest way to start. The people close to you don't think you're for real. They think you're just having fun. Your acquaintances laugh at you. And strangers, they don't want to know you at all.

There was no doubt: I was bad at selling. But the important point wasn't that I was failing (over and over again). The vital point was that I figured out *why* I was bad at it.

In the mid-1960s a friend of mine took this same three-day test for Hornblower. He was a manufacturer, had made a lot of money, owned a lot of investments. But he failed the test. He could sell a shirt but he couldn't sell an intangible, such as insurance or a stock.

I had learned at least two requirements for selling an intangible. First, you've got to have a story. The story is how you make it real to the prospective client. You fit your intangible into their way of thinking. That life insurance policy isn't just a policy, it's a story of what if – what if your meeting in the city runs late and the paperwork runs later but you don't want to miss your kid's baseball game the next day, what if you drive home to Loch Sheldrake at two in the morning, what if you're falling asleep and there's construction on the road and the wheel veers toward a cement blockade, what if you kept your money in the bank for six months, twelve months, getting average interest, but it was the wrong twelve months because at the end of the year there you are, driving into cement....

Second, you have to find out something about the person you're talking to. That story wouldn't work for a man who doesn't work late hours in the city. In the same way, an airline's stock won't work for someone who lives and dies by AT&T. The correct answer to the test question above is (d) Ask the client. Always, always ask first.

But that's just the elementary question in that scenario. You move up to the advanced level when you understand that an airline's stock might be *perfect* for an AT&T shareholder – if you know that he owns AT&T. Once he's confided that to you, you also know that he is a conservative investor with an interest in sectors of the economy that depend on consumer use, use that can only increase in the future. People use phones; people use airlines. The more time and money they have, the more they will use both. AT&T had cornered the market (at that time) so you don't want to present an airline that's a scrappy upstart in the thick of the fight of competition. But an airline that has good earning power and is actively using opportunities for growth – even a conservative AT&T shareholder can hear that argument.

End of story? Nope. You get to know everything about that prospective client, his birthday, children's birthdays, likes and dislikes. You talk to him on the phone five or six times before you start talking purchases. You get personal. You become that person's friend, and that was how we did business long before Facebook. Retail companies are very concerned with their social networking presence today; employees send personal emails to customers, tweet to them on Twitter, even tweet about them, giving them a little spotlight. New technology; old approach. Only when you have created a mutually sustaining relationship do you make your real selling pitch.

End of story? Nope. I can't tell you how many excellent presentations I have witnessed, bull's-eye sales pitches with the best prospects for success – and then the presenter doesn't ask for the order. So they don't get the order.

It sounds almost offensively simple: "So, how many shares would you like to have?" But it's the most important step and it is incredibly difficult to do, because it opens you to possible rejection.

Of course, over the last ten to thirty years a number of Wall Street brokers have been using a new sales approach: threaten the prospective client. Make him afraid of how much money he will lose if he doesn't buy this *incredible deal* – such as a bond made up of home mortgages. Make him feel like an idiot for passing up this opportunity. Make him feel like a scrawny nerd in a gym full of football stars if he doesn't buy your stock or bond or whatever you're selling. Make him feel like a coward. Bully him.

I don't hold with that. That's a nasty way to do business and it's a terrible way to run an economy.

Maybe that's one of the reasons why the brokerages stopped hiring companies to give this kind of test. Those companies were expensive, and future graduates now take personality tests such as the Myers-Briggs test at college. But I wonder: was this kind of test also too constraining? Did the brokerages want to hire employees who don't ask, who don't sell – who only manipulate and force? The sales figures go up astronomically – but at what cost?

After that second round of testing, I knew I had something to say that was worth hearing. By the time I reached the end of my long train ride home, I knew that I no longer needed this job. I wanted it.

* * *

My throat was not closed on the third day of testing. The psychologist was still crisp and neutral, but he was more personal now. He had to be. He was asking about my husband, my children, my life. Why was I interested in this job? Why was I anxious to do this job? Two separate questions, those. How would a job like this affect my family? How would they be taken care of?

I couldn't tell what he was looking for. I knew he was searching but would I know if he found it? I was really selling myself as an intangible – but I didn't know anything about the client I was selling to.

I didn't tell him I was having trouble with Sam. I did tell him that I was anxious to do this job because I needed money for my family. I felt I had aptitude for it – math skills, the ability to read a balance sheet. Yes, I was concerned about how to take care of my family; I didn't have a wife at home. My salary would have to pay someone to stay home full-time with the children. I had been thinking about these things for months and I made sure he knew that. He was probably making sure that I wasn't fly-by-night. I had thought through everything and I was serious.

I was so serious that when I found out the test results wouldn't be available for a month, I was too eager to wait. Earl suggested I research other brokerages with training programs. I found them and then I went and took those three days of tests all over again, for Shearson, Hammill & Company.

A few weeks later Earl called me. "My Senior Manager wants to meet with you. I think you must have done very nicely on the test."

At last! He was going to hire me, I just knew it. I forgot all about Shearson, Hamill & Company. I would rather work with Earl.

I had met Earl's Senior Manager once before, when I first asked if I could apply to join the training program. He was a slight man with fair hair, a little guarded when we first met. But now, with my test results in his hand, he gave me a warm smile when I sat down in his office.

"You did very well on the tests," he said, and moved right into explaining the salary. During the six months of the program the trainee would draw salary until taking the test for the license to sell stocks. After that, there would be a commission structure.

"But you know," he continued, "we're having a predicament. We would consider hiring you, but we've never hired a woman before and we have no idea what to pay you."

My throat closed up.

I was stunned.

I had no idea how many other women were in the industry – or how few. It never occurred to me that I might be the only one. I had felt like any other applicant but with one sentence, he separated me, he made me different. He made me female.

And he was telling me that because I was female, he was going to pay me less than the other stockbrokers.

Does this sound out of date? Yet there's every indication that women are still at a pay disadvantage because they don't negotiate their salaries in the same way that men do. The distinction is not as crude as the one this Senior Manager presented to me, but it's there and it has consequences. And women are not the only ones affected. A man who is less assertive for any reason, whether culturally or by temperament, is also at a disadvantage. Business – especially this industry – rewards aggressiveness at the expense of other character traits.

I'm not against aggressiveness; it was about to save my life. But when we wake up in 2008 and risk-taking daredevil day traders have aggressively gambled away our nation's wealth.... Someone has to be in charge of keeping the balance, of noticing when we've tipped too far in one direction or another.

My throat wasn't closed for long.

"I guess you want me to work part-time?" I said.

"No, I expect you to work full-time like everybody else."

"Then you can pay me like everybody else."

"But –"

"Why is this an issue, aren't you paying the men?"

"Yes, but they have wives –"

"They have wives, I have to hire a wife."

"They have families, expenses –"

"I have to hire someone to stay full-time with my baby and to be there when my sons get home from school. I have to take the same subways as the men, rent the same cars, buy a new wardrobe, too. I am not here for fun. I am here to work and the salary is very important to me and the commissions are even more important to me."

That was just the preamble. I talked for five minutes straight, ushering this Senior Manager into reality. Those months I spent examining my cinder-block cell while waiting to take the test – they had prepared me.

When I finished spitting fire – spitting all those sharpened pencils I'd swallowed during months of anxiety – the Senior Manager said, "Well I didn't think of it that way."

No, I guess he hadn't.

"How much do you think you'd like to make?"

"I have no limit," I said. "I want to make as much as I am capable of making. If I had a limit, I wouldn't be in this job, I'd take a secretary job."

He sat back and took that in.

"You know," he said, "I'm glad we're hiring you. You could sell the Brooklyn Bridge!"

It was an old joke even then, but that was the proudest moment of my life... so far.

Then and Now

The first bill that President Obama signed into law was the Lilly Ledbetter Fair Pay Act, which gives workers more time to file lawsuits against companies who have been engaging in unfair salary practices. Of course, situations involving unequal treatment in salary usually involve women being paid less than men.

The bill became law in 2009 but it remained a contentious issue. Just as I was finishing this book, the Governor of Wisconsin, Scott Walker, repealed his state's version of the law.

Why would anyone oppose this law? Critics of it say that it will hurt businesses because it gives workers too much opportunity to file a lawsuit. But if a situation is unfair, shouldn't a worker be able to remedy it *at any time*? I am all in favor of small businesses, of course, having run two of them, but if your management choices are wrong, then your choices should be corrected. It's that simple.

I fought for the right to equal pay from the very start of my career. Women in the financial industry were expected to work the same hours at the same level of effort but not receive the same salary or the same perks and bonuses, such as eating in the social clubs' dining rooms. I was fortunate to have felt able to fight that from the beginning. A person who has been treated unequally for years may feel inhibited and overwhelmed, even scared, of the idea of fighting. They should have all the time they need to muster their courage and their resources – especially the funds they will need for lawyers' fees – so that they can fight.

That is common sense. So anyone who opposes that really does have a problem with women's rights, specifically. I'm sad to say that I'm not surprised that the law has opponents. Women's equality is so much further along than it was fifty years ago, but in some ways we still aren't finished with the fight.

For example, every CEO of IBM has always been invited to become a member of the Augusta National Golf Club in Georgia, since IBM is one of its major sponsors. The club is especially prestigious because it hosts the annual Masters Tournament, one of only four championship games in golf. In 2011 IBM appointed a woman, Virginia Rometty, as CEO. The men's-only golf club didn't invite her to join – and still hasn't.*

That's asinine, it really is. Everyone knows how much business is conducted over the game of golf. Barring women from that shuts the same door as, once upon a time, barring women from the floor of the New York Stock Exchange did. And you can be sure that the mentality expressed in that club's rules is continued and acted upon outside the club, too.

Then there are the golf tournaments themselves, still segregated. Larry and I learned how to golf about five years ago and we belong to a golf club in Encino. There is a woman at our club who is an excellent golfer, far better than most of the men; yet she is not allowed to compete in the Masters Tournament because it is men's-only. That simply does not make sense. It is time for the rule-makers to change their minds.

---

* Note: As this book was being formatted, in August 2012 the Augusta National Golf Club announced that they were adding to their roster their first two female members: Condoleezza Rice and Darla Moore. Better late than never! I'm thrilled that they are making Progress at last.

CHAPTER FOUR
Knowing My Purpose

"YOU'RE CASTRATING ME!" Sam roared.

That shocked me out of my temper. We'd been fighting for an hour. I'd told him I was entering the training program. As I expected, he blew his top. An hour later my throat was raw from fighting with a lowered voice, but Sam's volume just kept going up. He had run out of arguments and was repeating himself for the third or fourth time.

"What will the families think? That you should go out of the home and work! None of my family have working wives! Neither does yours! What will the neighbors say? All the neighborhood mothers stay home! What are you going to do with the children, my god?!"

"I'll hire a full-time housekeeper, Sam."

"How am I going to afford that, are you crazy? You're crazy!"

I had mentioned before that I'd have a salary as a trainee, but I hadn't said how much. This time around, I told him. My trainee's salary was more than what he was making after fifteen years in the garment industry.

That's when he called me a ballbreaker.

What can you say to that?

With shock came calm. My temper folded. I walked away.

He didn't dare forbid me from taking the job. I didn't have that personality and he knew it. But I knew his personality. I knew he wasn't finished.

* * *

One good thing about the fight with Sam: it erased the memory of the Hornblower manager trying to underpay me. That incident could have rattled me. Instead, I walked into the sunny trainees' lecture room on my first day feeling clear and focused. Optimism can collapse under pressure, but knowing your purpose – that's reliable. My purpose was to build a long-term career. I had no upper limit and I wanted to make as much money as I was capable of making.

I was the only woman in a room full of men, but I didn't feel odd. Look, when you're five feet tall, everyone is intimidating. Until you get used to it, and then no one is intimidating. That stopped bothering me years before.

None of the men were paying attention to me anyway. They were thinking about their careers just as I was.

Then Joe Jackson walked into the room. He didn't sit with us; he went to the front of the room and stayed standing. We snapped out of our self-absorption and focused on him.

Joe was a tall man and unabashed about it. He didn't collapse his chest to shrink himself down. He was personable, too. He had been a stockbroker, but I think he was happier teaching because it brought him face to face with us. Brokers spend most of their time on the phone.

Someone must have told him I'd be there because he showed no surprise at the only woman who had ever entered the training program. His eyes didn't even hesitate on me as he learned our names. That would have been discourteous, and *that* wouldn't have been Joe Jackson.

Later, as we broke for coffee after our first class, the other students were realizing for the first time that I was there. They were courteous, too, but their looks noted me. Joe said to us all, "If you ever need help, don't hesitate to call me." With the smallest of glances, he conveyed that message twice over to me. He had my back, no matter what.

The training program would last six months, culminating in the exam for our New York Stock Exchange licenses. During the program we would spend several weeks in every department of Hornblower & Weeks. We were going to get a complete picture of how the firm operated, including how they executed orders for stocks and handled clients' accounts.

The stock market can be mystifying. Over the last thirty years, various personalities on Wall Street have discovered that if they make the process even more mystifying, they can make even more money. So I'll demystify the process.

A stock is ownership. When you buy a company's stock, you own a portion of that company. Your stock represents your share. Whatever the company earns in the future, you receive your proportionate share of those earnings as dividends.

A savvy investor will look at all aspects of a company to figure out its true value. The goal is to identify whether the company is likely to do well in the future and increase in value. If that is likely, the investor checks the price of the stock. The price may be low compared to the value of the company. If so, the stock is undervalued and that's a good time to buy the stock. If the price is too high, the stock is overvalued. That's not a good time to buy, but it may be a great time for a shareholder to sell.

Before buying a stock, a savvy investor will also look at the risk/reward of a stock – the chances of a loss and whether that would be temporary, versus the size and likelihood of profit down the road. If the investor can handle the risk, if the reward will probably be worth it, and if the stock price is good, it's time to buy.

Most of the movement in the stock market is shareholders buying and selling stocks to other shareholders, through stockbrokers. People make the stock market.

That's important enough to say twice. *People make the market.* "Wall Street" is only a means to an end. People determine what the end is.

Different people have different goals. The people who make and move the market tend to have investing philosophies. One major philosophy is the investor's view. An investor thinks long-term. An investor wants to hold a stock – own a portion of a company – for several years, sometimes for many years.

The other major philosophy is the short-term trader's view. A short-term trader doesn't care about the value of a company, only the stock price. He wants to buy and sell stocks as quickly as he can for the highest profits. He buys stock in the morning and sells it before the closing bell. His fast pace is exciting and it may result in high profits, but one poor choice can result in a massive loss.

Whichever philosophy the majority of shareholders chooses can change the overall behavior of the market.

My clients and I were (and still are) investors. We thought long-term and comprehensively. My job as an Account Executive (stockbroker) at Hornblower & Weeks was to manage my clients' portfolios. (A portfolio is all of the assets a client owns in the market.) I was a strategist: I recommended which stocks and bonds to buy and sell, and when to buy and sell them. I always kept my eye on the true value of the companies and the true needs of my clients. Long-term portfolios for my clients meant a long-term career for me, and that's exactly what I eventually had.

True value and true needs: that was the Old Wall Street. The life cycle of a sale depended on both.

How did I determine true value? Well, picking a stock is like candling an egg. You try to shed some extra light on a company so you can see exactly what's inside it. The men who candled the eggs at Hornblower were the Analysts. Their division was my favorite. I visited them every Monday morning for about ten years, even though my office was in Midtown and theirs was downtown in Hanover Square. "Here comes Norma!" they'd say. "It must be Monday!"

They were responsible for determining which stocks were worth buying and selling. They explained their recommendations to me so I could explain them to a client. An analyst usually had a master's degree in economics and he was a strategist, too. He would pick an industry and not just research everything about it, but really think through all the information that was available to him. He would try to predict growth potential for the companies within the industry. The analysts called their industry contacts every day to keep their information about the industry up to date. They wrote reports, too, but I never skimped on the opportunity to talk to them in person. I needed to know exactly what I was selling.

Once I knew the stocks I wanted my clients to buy, I had to choose which clients were suitable for each stock. To do that, I needed to know my clients' true needs. That means getting personal with a client, building a real relationship.

And just like a first date, the very first conversation I had with any potential client carried a lot of weight.

Almost all of those first conversations were cold calls. No one was going to hand me clients; I had to find my own. That meant talking to strangers, and our training program spent a whole month teaching us how to do that. (It was the last month of the program. We learned how to cold call, we got our licenses, then we leaped right back into cold calling. They didn't want us to forget it!)

Cold calling included phoning anyone who might have an interest in investing. Sometimes I'd hear about someone through a friend or an acquaintance. Sometimes I just went through the phone book. (I'm not exaggerating.) Cold calling also included cold visiting: walking into an office full of people who had no idea who I was and asking to speak to the person in charge of investments. Cold calling is, in a word, terrifying.

But oh, I learned it. I learned it the easy way: by Joe Jackson giving me good advice and by practicing it on my colleagues in the classroom. What's the first thing I say on the phone? How can I tell if someone is interested or just being polite? If they're not interested, when do I end the phone call? How can I end it in a way that might leave the door open for later? I walk into an office and a secretary greets me. How do I treat her? Remember, she's my best chance to meet the principals of that firm. If she's less than helpful the first time I meet, how many more times do I drop in and try again?

And I learned it the hard way: by doing it. Since I had sold insurance and mutual funds before, at least the nervousness was familiar. Some of the other guys in the class had trouble adjusting. The competitiveness among us really started to come out. A successful cold call meant that now you had a prospective client. After five or six calls to that person – after you built a relationship – you could discuss making a specific purchase of a stock. If that went well, you had a client. The better your cold calling skills, the more clients you could have.

Among my colleagues in the training program I felt like a regular competitor. OK, one of the better ones. I was even learning to love making cold calls and cold visits. But the competition wasn't the same for me as it was for them. Most of the time when I called a stranger and introduced myself, I'd hear, "Come on, there's no such thing as a lady stockbroker! You're a salesgirl working from home, don't try and fool me."

I couldn't blame them for being mistaken. At that time women making business calls usually were, in fact, working from home and selling cosmetics or housecleaning products. So I had to gently, firmly correct my potential clients before I could even talk business. That's an awkward way to begin a relationship. I had to convince them that I was legitimate.

More often than not, I'd find the humor in the situation and that would keep them on the phone. My book of potential clients grew steadily, and I was one of the top contenders in the unofficial cold calling competition.

The misconceptions of the men I cold called – well, that was unfair, but I could only change their minds after we started talking. In every other situation during the Hornblower training program, I required fair treatment. I never forgot being segregated with Nona Vieja at the synogogue when I was a little girl. Most of the time my requirement went unchallenged in the training program, but sometimes I had to fight for it.

Interspersed with our tutorials and our observation stints in the different departments were lectures from the Best in the Business. Joe Jackson brought them in mostly from the ranks of Hornblower, so those lectures occurred in our trainees' room. One day Joe made an announcement: an esteemed dignitary from the New York Stock Exchange would be happy to speak to us at his social club. But there was one problem. The very exclusive, high-class men's social club did not allow women in its dining room. Since I was in the class, they had reserved the small ladies' lunchroom for all of us instead.

The claws came out. My classmates erupted. No way did they want to be shuffled off to the side like that. To miss the opportunity to be inside one of those social clubs, you're kidding! I knew they wanted to smell the leather of the seats, the smoke of the cigars. They wanted to be able to brag about this for months. And so did I! I would be as deprived of the experience as they would. But my colleagues were not "all for one." They were adamant: I was going to have to miss this lunch so they could sit in the club's dining room.

"Norma," Joe said, "can I see you outside for a moment?"

We stepped into the hallway.

"What do you think?" he said.

"You want me to stay home?" I asked.

"No!"

"Then they can sit in the ladies' lunchroom with me," I said, and went back inside.

Joe followed me in, announced that the class would sit in the ladies' lunchroom, and changed the topic before everyone could start blowing steam again.

After the class, though, I received a number of sour looks. When Joe had left the room, one of my fellow trainees said to me, "Why are you here? You're taking a job that could go to a man with a family to feed. We all have families. We all have reasons to be here. That's a selfish thing to do, Norma."

"I have a family, too," I replied. Then I got a little snotty with him. He'd earned it.

I continued to get sour looks, especially the day we sat down in that ladies' lunchroom of the social club, but the comments stopped, even when other lectures occurred in other social club lunchrooms. I had shown that I would defend myself. They began to respect me even though I was a woman.

* * *

There was no ladies' lunchroom at home, though – no compromise available. And selfishness was Sam's favorite refrain. "The family doesn't need the money! My salary is enough! You're selfish for taking this job. You're working to make yourself happy. You're greedy for money for yourself and you're using your family as an excuse. You are so selfish, you are sacrificing *your children* to this job. Disgusting!"

Coming home from the city, I never knew if my house would be on fire. Some nights Sam would be silent. Other nights, he'd be raging and roaring. Or one of our relatives would call after he'd complained to them and go on the attack. Even my parents didn't think I was doing right by the children.

"Left alone and suffering," Sam put it. "Our poor kids. You're a terrible mother."

I had provided full-time care for my children but Sam knew how to get to me. He knew my soft spot. I went to bed feeling guilty every night for years.

* * *

I felt guilty not just because of the children, but because I *was* happy at Hornblower. I hadn't been this happy since Wisconsin, almost fifteen years ago. I could not wait to make a real sale but of course, until I earned my license, I was still learning everything in theory.

I had my book of potential clients; I had the stocks the Analysts recommended. The next step of a sale would be to consult my clients' files. I had to make sure the stock aligned with a client's interests and true needs. I would also consult the Margin Department. I realized during the training program that working closely with that department would be a good idea. They would calculate the worth of my clients' holdings and their buying power – how much each client could borrow from Hornblower to invest. If the value of a client's stock holdings had increased because the stocks he owned had increased in price, then he could borrow more to buy more. This is called leveraging and it's similar to a homeowner borrowing money against the equity of his house.

However, in the stock market a client must maintain his margin position – the value of his assets as compared to how much he has borrowed – so that he maintains his ratio of debt to assets. If the prices of his stocks decrease, he either has to add cash or more assets to his account or sell stocks until he has lowered his debt. Hornblower's Margin Department had to check that every client was maintaining his margin position, as well as compute his buying power. Now we have computers but then, the Margin Department did all those complex calculations by hand.

In the next step of a sale, I would call the client and describe the company to him. (Clients were almost never women then. Women weren't allowed to open checking accounts or have credit cards without their husband's signatures, let alone brokerage accounts. Even when I became a licensed stockbroker, Hornblower did not allow me to have my own account without my husband's permission. I wouldn't dare to ask Sam for that. Eventually Earl Rubin approved my application to open my account, but it took a while.)

If the client were interested in the stock, he'd ask for a quote of the current stock price. I'd tell him I would call him back. Then I called on a party line – one phone line shared by everyone in my office at Hornblower – to get a quote. They put me on hold. Eventually, after I waited for other people on the party line to finish their business, I received my answer. I called the client back and he made his decision. If he said yes, I would (once I earned my license) hand-write an order to purchase stock, walk to the back of our department's room, and hand it to the order clerk. He would teletype it to our main office downtown. The main office would place the order in a steel cartridge and insert it into a pneumatic tube. There were 55 miles of pneumatic tubes in the city, underground; our tube would swish my order to the floor of the New York Stock Exchange.

One of our representatives at the Hornblower booth would grab my order and hurry through the thrashing, bellowing crowd to find the market maker for that particular stock. The market maker was in charge of The Book, a ledger book that tracked the trades between buyers and sellers of that stock. He would execute my order by matching the closest buyer and seller. Then he would record it in The Book and report it back to Hornblower. The sale would be complete.

Slips of paper, pneumatic tubes, ledger books: archaic technology, obviously. Computers did away with all of this. So why bother going over it?

Because being voice-to-voice with the client, the phone operators, the men who gave me quotes, my colleagues sharing my phone line who could hear what I was saying, the order clerk – all this human contact reminded us that Wall Street was fundamentally a human enterprise.

Some people on Wall Street needed that reminder more than others, I discovered during the training program. I never expected to find a similarity between the New York Stock Exchange and my parents' card game parties, but then I ran into the Exchange's Board of Governors.

Naturally the two weeks that we were going to observe the floor of the Exchange were going to be a highlight of our training program. Joe Jackson's announcement that we were headed to the floor of the Exchange was greeted with great excitement.

"Norma, can I see you outside a moment?" Joe added.

Hallways certainly do see a lot of bad news.

"The members of the Board of Governors don't allow women on the floor of the Exchange."

Oh boy. Here we go.

"Why *not*?"

"I've been arguing with them for a few days and I've gotten three answers. The knee-jerk answer is, it just hasn't been done."

"Then it's time to do it."

"Well, the unofficial answer, and I'm not supposed to be telling you this, is that women are considered bad luck."

"They're *superstitious*? What is this, a ship? Are we in the Navy now?"

"Yeah, even they know that one doesn't hold water."

"Ha ha."

"So the third answer is, there are no ladies' lounges on the Exchange."

"Bathrooms, Joe, just say bathrooms. OK, so I'll use the men's bathroom."

"Norma –"

"I'll get one of our guys to stand watch while I'm in there. Problem solved."

I went back inside. Joe delivered the message.

The Board demurred. The Board fumed. But the Board did not get their way. I showed up every day before the stock market opened to use the toilets, with a colleague to stand watch. And then I walked that world-famous floor, littered with crumpled slips of paper and untouched by women's heels. The New York Stock Exchange, center of the financial world, bent down to extend the gangplank for me. And about time, too.

Bad luck? Phooey!

For all the women who waited until a card game was finished to sneak away to the toilet; for all the women who never dreamed they could be more than salespeople working from home; for all the women who couldn't own credit cards; and for all the young women now who have never had to deal with those problems – I walked the floor of the Exchange for you.

And after those two weeks, I didn't spend much time there. I wasn't interested in that side of the business and I had made my point. And the Board of Governors never forgot it.

* * *

"Mommy?" I was home, taking off my coat and heels in the hallway. Four-year-old Elysa was watching.

"Yes, honey?"

"Daddy said you go to work because you don't love us."

I just sat down on the stairs and cried.

Sam's latest trick: twist the knife in the kids. It worked better than he could have imagined. Victor and Stephen weren't as verbal with me as Elysa, my poor little girl who thought what her daddy said was true. The behavior of the boys changed, though. Their grades started to slip. Stephen started skipping school. And it broke my heart to see them try to hide in their bedrooms when Sam and I fought elsewhere in the house. The walls were not thick enough to keep our harshness away from them.

I hoped, I deeply hoped, that things would change when I had my license.

* * *

The training program was in its last month. The day of the licensing exam was approaching. It was cold calling season and we were working as hard as we could, hoping to have a solid book of clients to work with as soon as we were licensed. Many of my colleagues were working the friends of friends and distant relatives angle. I was looking around, thinking, wondering....

It occurred to me that Park Avenue near Earl's office might be a good place to do some cold calling. One day after lectures in the morning, I headed up there to practice. At the end of the day I'd be reporting back to Joe Jackson and my colleagues about my results.

I started on Park Avenue, then eventually worked my way over to Fifth Avenue. I spent a few minutes looking into the windows of Harry Winston, the jeweler. He'd always been a sensation, and just a few years previously he had donated the Hope Diamond to the Smithsonian.

What if I walked in there...

Well why shouldn't I?

I mean, aside from the sheer, chilling terror of cold calling one of the most famous jewelers in the world.

I located the entrance to their offices and walked up. I introduced myself to the receptionist, very nicely, and asked to speak to the person who handled Mr. Winston's investments. She gave me an odd look and I knew what she was thinking: a lady stockbroker? You're kidding.

But she made a call, then ushered me into the office of a private secretary, a woman. I had no idea who she was, but chutzpah had gotten me this far.

"Hello," I said. "I'm a trainee at the brokerage firm Hornblower & Weeks, and it's my job to cold call prospective clients. I'd like to know a little bit about Mr. Winston's investments so that when I pass my exam and get my sales license, I could work with his investment managers."

Please, please, let the direct honesty approach work....

The private secretary, it turned out, managed Mr. Winston's investments. But she was a woman! This time it was my turn to be shocked.

"I'm very impressed," Harry Winston's investment manager said, "that they're starting to train women for the stock market. We do have some brains!"

She gave me the names of three companies. "Whatever you see or hear about these companies, call me and let me know."

So I put her in my tickler file. I made an absolute pest of myself hounding my friends the Analysts for information on those three companies. I called her with whatever information I could get. And when I passed my exam and acquired my license, she gave me an order for one of those stocks.

I thought I was aiming toward one goal: my license, listing me as Norma Hason Nahmias at the New York Stock Exchange in 1962. But by the time I got there, another achievement had overshadowed that one. The coup of a rookie broker getting an order for Harry Winston was the headline of the whole training program.

* * *

Almost twenty years later Joe Jackson visited me, founder and president of Yaeger Securities, my brokerage firm in Los Angeles. He was retiring and had decided to look me up while he was on the West Coast. We had a grand talk and toward the end, Joe started crying.

"Joe? Joe, are you OK?"

"Oh yes, yes." He wiped his eyes. "It's just a pleasure to see one of my students who made it."

Joe Jackson, thank you.

A Word About Wall Street

There is such a difference between the market then and the market now that they almost deserve different names. The Old Wall Street that I started out in... must sound quaint. Or maybe it sounds impossible. New Wall Street began to depart from the old ways about twenty years ago.

We are just starting to see what the major consequences are from all the different choices that have been made, and are still being made.

Plenty of investors still exist in the stock market now, thinking and planning for the long term. But on the New Wall Street, there are more and more people with a short-term philosophy. The speed of computer transactions tempts people who by temperament and by need *should* be investors, to be short-term traders instead.

The short-term trading approach was of no interest to me. My goal was long-term career success, not just quick, wild successes. Some of these brokers on New Wall Street approach their careers like they only have five or six years to make as much money as they can. I made choices that added decades to my career. I saw my clients as partners, very much so. I genuinely liked people, and this career let me meet them and learn about them and get a feel for all the different kinds of people out there. It was easy for me to be loyal to my clients.

On New Wall Street, many brokers see their clients as a means to an end. That mindset leads to greed and *un*ethical behavior. They forget that their clients are people.

Computers have done this. The age of computers has changed the personal relationship between broker and client. In my early years at Hornblower & Weeks, I was always reminded that I was working with people. I had a team: my colleagues, as well as my clients. When I started in the training program, the only technology we had was our party-line, rotary-dial telephone. You got things done with the help of other people or they didn't get done. You had to have patience and you had to have courtesy. You had respect for everyone. You were reminded all the time that Wall Street is a human enterprise.

In this age of computers, New Wall Street has not found a new way to remind all of its employees of that.

Speculative brokers are a prime example of this. Now, speculation is not inherently a bad thing. An ethical speculative broker may suggest a chancy stock to a client, but first the broker will examine the risk/reward of the stock. The broker will only suggest a high-risk stock to a client who can handle a lot of risk. The broker will always make it clear to the client that the stock price may easily go down tomorrow instead of up. The future reward, though, may be worth the risk.

Speculative brokers don't always start with chancy stocks, either. Sometimes they advise a client to buy stock in a worthwhile company at a stock price that accurately represents the true value of the company. Then the speculative brokers drive up the price by getting as many other clients as possible to buy the stock.

But there is a line between ethical and unethical speculating. A speculative broker who forgets that clients and colleagues are people, who sees them only as means to an end, may also forget his or her ethics.

An unethical speculative broker will drive people to buy chancy stocks *without* informing them of the risk. The broker may not *ever* examine the risk/reward of a stock, just drive people to buy it even if its price is wildly overvalued, completely divorced from the true value of the company. An *un*ethical speculative broker will convince clients to use as much of their buying power as possible to buy a risky stock, ignoring the possibility that the stock price may decline, which would force the clients to add cash or sell stocks to maintain their margin. All of these actions by the broker boost the stock price higher, but they put clients in precarious positions.

Speculative brokers, both ethical and unethical, some-times concentrate on a particular industry. They drive up the stock prices for all of the companies within an industry. (They don't get together and decide to do this; it's not a conspiracy. But a broker will get the idea to drive up prices, another broker will copycat, a few more will follow their lead, and then a whole bunch of brokers will jump on the bandwagon.) If there's a boom – millions and millions of dollars being invested in those stocks at those high prices – then a bubble forms.

The bubble lasts until one of the large institutional investors who owns millions of dollars' worth of that stock decides to sell at a high, overvalued price. Other major investors see that sale and think they should sell, too, reaping those profits. They start selling stocks across the entire industry. But they sell too much, too fast. The stock prices for that industry slip. Many people who bought those stocks on margin won't have enough cash to add to their assets – they are overleveraged – so they have to sell, too. That starts an avalanche.

Everyone panics and sells until the sellers run out of buyers. The stock prices plummet. The stock market as a whole won't crash, but the bubble in that industry bursts. Sometimes the stocks in related industries slide, too. And a lot of people lose a lot of money.

The boom and bust cycle occurred occasionally on the Old Wall Street, and we had our speculative brokers, too. On the New Wall Street, however, the boom and bust cycle is happening more frequently. The consequences of the speculative brokers' actions are greatly magnified.

One reason is that there are more people in the stock market now. On the Old Wall Street, public awareness of the market was limited. Now we have more private investors, more institutions, more pension plans, more speculative brokers, and more of every kind of shareholder, including more shareholders with a short-term mentality.

The other reason is that computers allow all those people to buy and sell at lightning speed. On the Old Wall Street, only a limited number of orders could be processed. Any risky behavior was at least slowed down. On New Wall Street there is less time for thought, consideration, and ethics.

There are also fewer regulations now, because people said they didn't want Big Government. But regulations are good for the market: they cut back on a great deal of speculation. Without them, New Wall Street has fewer brakes on risky behavior.

And there is so much more money circulating in the market now. This has made possible a new breed of risky speculative broker: one who makes trades not for private investors, but for his or her brokerage firm. The money used for trading isn't the broker's or a client's, but the firm's. A big brokerage firm has so much money, it can seem like its resources are inexhaustible (though they aren't). A big brokerage firm also might not thoroughly oversee the actions of its brokers, although it is the firm's responsibility to do so. A broker bringing in money should be held responsible for how that's done. It can be very easy for a broker to forget to examine risk/reward and just hurtle recklessly forward.

The extraordinary amounts of money available and the few restrictions allow these speculative brokers to form bubbles over multiple industries, not just one. When multiple bubbles pop, a country's economy can collapse. Everyone suffers.

The Great Recession that began with the market crash in 2008 was a priceless learning opportunity. That was the moment for us to re-learn the lessons about why and how to regulate speculators in the financial industry, and Congress did pass some regulations. However, some extremely influential people apparently learned nothing at all. Jamie Dimon was one of them.

Mr. Dimon was and is President and CEO of JP Morgan Chase, one of the most powerful brokerage-banks in the world. JP Morgan is the brokerage side of the company; Chase is the bank side. The Glass-Steagall Act, made into law after the Great Depression, had decreed that banks and brokerage firms should always be separate entities, but that was repealed in 1999. This means that funds deposited in the bank side of a brokerage-bank are not necessarily safe. If the brokerage side of a brokerage-bank makes hugely risky investments and loses so much that the brokerage side fails, the bank depositors' capital will be at risk, too.

That is not fair. People deposit money in banks because it's supposed to be safe there.

The highly risky practices of the big brokerage firms, including the brokerage-banks, leading up to the 2008 market crash made it clear that something had to be done about the unbridled opportunity of those firms to take risks. The regulations put into place after 2008 included the Volcker Rule, which was supposed to limit the most speculative types of trading for brokerage-banks, thus limiting the amount of risk they could incur.

The head honchos of New Wall Street hated the Volcker Rule, and its most vocal opponent was Jamie Dimon. Because JP Morgan Chase was so highly regarded, his arguments were heeded. Loopholes were added to the Volcker Rule that allowed brokerage-banks to continue to engage in some speculative behavior such as proprietary trading.

Well, one afternoon in May 2012, Jamie Dimon made a little announcement. The brokerage side of JP Morgan Chase had lost two billion dollars in speculative trading.

Two billion dollars.

Using the very loopholes in the Volcker Rule that Mr. Dimon had lobbied for.

Current investigations are now estimating that the loss may even be as great as four billion dollars.

Now, if Jamie Dimon's brokers had lost half a million dollars, no one would have cared. And JP Morgan Chase has so much money that neither its brokerage side nor its bank side are in danger of failing. But a system that allows a two billion dollar loss is a broken system. Jamie Dimon and his brokers were so arrogant that they thought they could write the law so that the law did not apply to them – that no matter how big a disaster they caused, the consequences would not be severe. Some of Dimon's brokers lost their jobs, but it remains to be seen whether Dimon and his firm will receive punishment that fits what should have been a crime.

If the government doesn't regulate people like that, who will?

Government can't be the only force of change in the financial industry, though. The public needs to do its share, too. It can't accomplish that if it is paralyzed with indecision or trying to alter the system radically from outside it.

I see that among the public, demonizing Wall Street and corporations is a growing trend. "Corporation" is almost a dirty word to some very angry, very scared people. Considering what speculative brokers and their short-term trading clients are continuing to do to our economy, this makes some emotional sense. But hiding your head in the sand is not a solution.

I say this: You should LOVE the market! I love the market! I still invest! And the reason I loved the Old Wall Street and why I still love the market now is that *people make the market*. They always did and they still do.

Not having computers on the Old Wall Street reminded us to be human and treat each other humanely. But we don't need to get rid of computers to restore that humanity. We just need to remember that we are people buying and selling with other people.

A corporation is an individual. Many people want the law that codified that idea to be struck down. But a corporation *is* made up of individuals. So instead of turning your back on investing and corporations altogether, why not treat companies like individuals in a very real way? Research a company. Get to know it. Figure out whether you'd like to be in a relationship with it for two to three years or longer. If the research looks positive to you, then invest in it. Be as conscientious buying stock in a company as if you were buying the whole company. And then be a partner in that relationship you have created.

In other words, care about companies.

Care about the people who work for them.

You, the investor, can restore the humanity to Wall Street. People have changed the behavior of the market toward more booms and busts – and bigger booms and bigger busts. But the more investors we have who do not behave like Jamie Dimon and his traders, the healthier the market will be. The more investors we have who think long-term, the more we can tip the balance of the market away from its current volatility. When the majority of shareholders are investors again, not short-term traders – when the majority of them behave ethically, not arrogantly – the behavior of the market will change back to something we can all live with.

CHAPTER FIVE
The Hat and Brooch Lady

OVER THE SIX months of my training program, my relatives had taken sides. There were the relatives who listened to Sam complain, then called me to tell me I was a terrible mother. There were the relatives who probably weren't against my career but were worried about the children, too. My parents were in that group, but they stayed pretty quiet about the whole thing. My sister Mildred and her husband David were my only relatives who were fully, vocally supportive.

Then there were the relatives I hadn't been in touch with and wasn't sure where they stood. I decided to find out about them. If they did support my career, they might be interested in being my clients. I started cold calling my family before Hornblower assigned me an office and a desk. I made my calls on the training program's phone.

One of the relatives I called was Matty (Matthew) Baker. A cousin of my father, he and his brother Jack owned a successful ladies' sportswear manufacturing firm. I told him I was nearing my licensing exam and would soon be executing transactions.

"Norma, that's wonderful!" he said. "I'm so proud of you!"

You know, I got a little emotional. I had family who was proud of me.

"So," he continued, "what are you going to wear?"

"Oh, I don't know, same as I was wearing in the training program. Skirts and blouses."

"So everyone will think you're a secretary," he said. "I know what a brokerage office looks like. You know how the secretaries sit right next to the stockbrokers?"

I thought about the huge Hornblower & Weeks brokers' room that we'd spent two weeks observing. It was on Park Avenue between 51st Street and 52nd Street, across from the Waldorf Astoria. The north half of the building was leased to the Mosler Safe Company, so there were giant industrial safes and bank vaults on display in all their windows. (I liked how that complemented our industry, too.)

The south half of the building was Hornblower's. Our office took up the whole ground floor, so it was the size of half a city block. It was also two stories tall with floor-to-ceiling windows. It wasn't just a fishbowl for the general public to casually glance into, though. This office was competing with all of New York City for the attention of that general public. It was designed to be so splendid, spacious, and dramatic that people would want to walk in and become involved with this amazing adventure known as the stock market. Our office had to look successful and it did.

In the front of the room was the scrolling ticker tape of every stock being traded and its current price. Below the tape was the board with every stock on the Dow Jones Industrial Average and their prices. The numbers were on panels that flicked up or down with a little *whap* sound every time a stock price changed, like an arrivals and departures board in a train station. The *whaps* of the panels, the hum of the tape – both would speed up when the volume of trading increased on the market. As they accelerated, like a caller at a horse race, the adrenalin in the room rose, too, especially for the brokers.

The back of the room was full of chairs for the general public to sit in when they came in to check the board or watch the tape to see how a particular stock was priced. They could also read the reports we'd provided on various stocks. And come they did; there was an almost constant flow of guests from Park Avenue.

Between the board and the public were the brokers and secretaries, arranged in pods: three brokers and one secretary to each pod of four desks.

"So," Matty interrupted. "Three men and one woman in each pod. Except at your pod, which will have two men and two women. How is anybody looking at your pod going to know which woman is the secretary?"

I saw his point. I'd already experienced people's incredulity on the phone. Why would it be different when they were looking at me in person? Women in brokerage offices were secretaries, that's what people thought. I was going to have to change everyone's minds, one mind at a time.

"Come visit me," Matty said. "Let's talk about this."

I sat down in Matty's office and he started talking.

"Norma, I'm going to help you be a great salesman," he said. "Saleswoman," he caught himself. "Now listen. If you want to be successful, you have to look successful. Here's what you're going to do. Go and get yourself a couple of walking suits."

"But –"

"I know you don't have the money, take a loan, borrow money, do anything, but get yourself some walking suits, you know, with the dress and matching jacket so you can walk outside in it or just wear the dress indoors. Also buy yourself leather gloves, fancy stockings, high-heeled shoes, purses to match the shoes, and hats. Don't forget the hats. You're to wear a hat at all times, you are never to take your hat off!"

"I don't know, Matty. Never?"

"Never! There may not be any lady stockbrokers but I know what the lady editors wear in the magazine industry, and they never take their hats off. You have good jewelry?"

I mentioned a few items.

"Good jewelry, Norma. Good jewelry."

"I have a little ruby and diamond ring my parents gave me in high school."

"Too small. But have the stones taken out and re-set as a brooch. You're going to be the Hat and Brooch Lady!"

"The Hat and Brooch Lady," I tried on the phrase.

"When people look in the office window to see the stock ticker I want them to see you and say, 'Who is that?!' You're different, Norma, you've got to stand out and look different!"

He wouldn't let me leave his office until I agreed. Matty always was a great salesman.

* * *

The loan officer stared at me.

"As a matter of procedure I do need to verify your employment," he said.

"I understand," I said.

75

He picked up the phone and called Hornblower & Weeks to find out if they really had just hired a woman as an Account Executive. He just didn't believe me when I said I was a stockbroker.

"Well," he said, hanging up the phone, "that's wonderful, congratulations!"

"Thank you!"

"Just to re-confirm, your husband *is* still currently working?"

Long story short, I got the thousand-dollar loan because I also had a working husband. It was doubtful whether I would have gotten the loan if I had been single.

But I didn't have time to dwell on that. I had a thousand dollars to invest in myself, and quickly.

It was the era of Jackie Kennedy, the woman who gave us a White House we could be proud of – but now, in 1964, a widow. The only bleak day I'd experienced during my training program was the day of JFK's assassination.

With Matty's help, her style became my style. My goal was to change people's minds before they even spoke to me. I selected three walking suits: black with Persian lamb collar and cuffs, camel-colored with mink collar and cuffs, and forest green with leopard fur collar and cuffs. (All that fur – it was different times then. I still have those collars and cuffs, well wrapped in a drawer.) I bought three pairs of leather gloves, an alligator skin purse, and a snakeskin purse. High-heeled shoes to match the purses, of course – and in those days, I wore the heels from dawn to dusk. There was no changing into athletic shoes for the walk to and from the subway. I chose three pillbox hats to match the collars and cuffs of the walking suits; and I picked up my new gold, ruby, and diamond brooch from the jeweler's.

When I walked into the Analysts' department on Monday morning, they didn't say "Here comes Norma!" They said, "Wow! Who's that lady? Norma?! Wow!!"

Even more gratifying was entering the brokers' office in midtown later that day. I had been placed under Earl Rubin's management. (The Senior Manager had joked, "He recommended you, now he's stuck with you!" And I'd laughed. I wouldn't have it any other way.) I looked around that splendid room, half a city block large, I heard the hum of the tape and the *whaps* of the prices on the board, and I knew that I looked as dramatic and splendid as my office. I noticed people outside on Park Avenue looking at me instead of at the stock ticker. I could see it on their faces: Who's that lady?!

Matty's plan was working. My outfits displayed a self-confidence that I hadn't fully developed yet but needed to exhibit. You have to sell yourself before you can sell anything to anyone.

And there came a day when a secretary led a stranger to the chair next to my desk that was available for clients. Ordinarily if a member of the general public asked to speak to a broker, he would be ushered over to the Broker of the Day. The brokers took turns in that position, according to alphabetical order. Walk-ins regularly became clients so I noticed the Broker of the Day frowning at me. This walk-in had asked for me specifically, though, so the Broker of the Day couldn't do anything about it.

This walk-in, it turned out, had been coming and going through our brokerage office for several days, sitting in the back of the room, reading some of our stock reports, and watching all of us brokers working.

"I realized you're a stockbroker by the outfit you're wearing," he said. (Thank you, Matty!) "I've been watching you work and you handle yourself well," he continued. "You're diligent, active, very ready to help. Would you mind if I gave you some of my stocks to research?"

Of course I was delighted.

If he had made a pass at me, because sometimes these wise guys would, I would have told him off right there in the office. That's how I always handled those situations. (Unless a man made a comment just off-the-cuff. Then I would simply say, "Thanks, that's very nice, but I'm not available." No sense in starting unnecessary battles.) But my walk-in client explained, "All of my professional people are women: my lawyer, my accountant, my doctor, my dentist. I respect the fact that a woman has to work twice as hard and do better than her male counterparts to make it."

He wasn't wrong about that. I set a standard of working extra hard during my first year and pushed myself to meet that standard throughout my career. In 1964 the market was still recovering from a downturn, so I was working with nervous, noncommittal clients as well as being brand new. I plugged away at my desk every minute, trying to restore their trust in the market again.

It helped that I was very organized and good on the phone. I was required to keep a book (a looseleaf notebook) tracking the dates and amounts of all my clients' purchases and sales. To that I added a tickler filing system I devised to keep track of all the other important information: birthdays, anniversaries, hobbies, wives' and children's names and interests. That helped me make every phone call a personal and positive experience, and enough of those phone calls created real relationships.

One of my clients, I talked to him for years but never met him. Then one year he invited me to his son's Bar Mitzvah. I showed up having no idea what my client looked like. He had no clue about me either. But the minute I opened my mouth, I heard "Norma! I knew that was you! I recognized your voice."

Everybody wants to be treated well, and on my side, I'd rather treat a client that way, too. It wouldn't be fun for me, either, talking endless business with someone I hardly knew.

I didn't stick to the phone, though. I knew cold visiting was as important as cold phone calls. Park Avenue, Madison Avenue, and Fifth Avenue had blocks and blocks of tall, stone buildings full of offices. I went through them one by one, floor by floor, office by office, walking in and introducing myself to strangers.

It was not easy. Rejection was my middle name. But also, rejection wasn't even in my vocabulary. If I had sat around worrying about how much I was getting rejected, I would have been ignoring all the opportunities that opened up from those visits, too. The more times you try, the better your chances for success, it's as simple as that.

After a while, cold visiting and cold calling started to feel more rewarding than terrifying. It began to feel like a game, how to persuade the secretaries to permit me access to the senior executives. My approach kept working! In the continuing competition with my colleagues I was doing extremely well. I was determined to prove Earl Rubin right for recommending me for Hornblower. Within a year, he and the Senior Manager were already impressed.

My competitiveness also helped my male colleagues understand that I was working on their level. So did my outfits! I was a professional and they knew they had to treat me that way. Disrespecting me was out of the question.

I heard in 1964 that certain members of Congress opposed to the Civil Rights bill had made a change to the wording: "That it shall be the policy of the United States to insure equal employment opportunities for Federal employees without discrimination because of race, color, religion, sex or national origin..." They had added the word "sex" because they felt sure that no one would pass civil rights for women, and therefore ethnic minorities wouldn't attain their civil rights either.

Phooey!

Yes, it's a silly word for a serious topic. But my ability to keep my good humor and equilibrium while at the same time tolerating no nonsense – that helped the men in this man's world adjust to my presence.

* * *

Home drained the good humor out of me, though. Sam refused to be mollified, refused to adjust and adapt. We were still fighting. I was trying to figure out a way to reduce the fights because I knew how they upset the children, but I didn't have any good ideas yet. The fights continued. The boys withdrew as much as they could.

Sometimes I think Elysa bore the worst of it. The housekeepers kept disappointing me, to say it mildly. One of them was a thief. Another one, I got a call from a neighbor, "Norma, I don't know why Elysa is walking up and down the street by herself, where's your housekeeper?" Well, the housekeeper had just gotten up and left. I know there are two sides to every story, maybe they had had a fight, but Elysa was only four years old.

And in November of 1965, the Northeast got hit with the Great Blackout and my neighbor called me to say that another housekeeper had abandoned Elysa. "Please take her in," I begged. The subways weren't working so I took a long bus ride to Queens, picked up my car from the subway station, and drove home without traffic lights, nearly crying all the way. My poor daughter.

All my guilt about my children spilled out during my sessions with Doc Grossman. More than once I wondered if I should quit my career. "No," he said. "There's only one way out of this box for you *and* your children. To take it, you must be financially independent from Sam. I'm not going to let you give up."

I knew he was right, but I couldn't even think the word "divorce" yet, let alone say it to anybody. In my family, divorce just didn't happen. But I couldn't remember the last kind word Sam and I had exchanged.

* * *

The trouble with the housekeepers was part of another trend, one I had not expected at all. As I said, once a man understood that I was a professional doing a professional's job, he usually wouldn't pull any nonsense. Not all of the women I encountered, though, were as helpful and interested as Harry Winston's private secretary had been.

I learned quickly not to call my clients when they were at home. If their wives answered they would get suspicious, even when I made a point of saying that I was a broker, not some "other woman." Better for me to catch the men in their offices.

The secretaries for the Accounts Executives were difficult, too. They didn't want to work with me. I was a tough boss, I admit it. I knew how I wanted things done and I wasn't shy about requiring it. There was something else going on, however. The secretaries didn't mind working for the tough male bosses. They might have been jealous; I was dressed like a peacock, after all, and earning commissions. But they also preferred men because they wanted to work for the most successful stockbrokers. That would give them higher bonuses and greater status. Even though I was doing so well, very much a contender with my colleagues, the secretaries had a basic assumption that no woman could be as successful as a man. It took a long time to find a secretary who didn't have that bias.

My good relationships with my clients more than made up for any other difficulties, though. Their conviviality would improve a hard day and in at least one case, came to my rescue.

One of my clients had put in a big order for thousands of shares of Eastern Airlines, selling at 30. A lot of money was on the line. At that time, clients could DVP their orders. DVP stands for Deliver Versus Payment: we delivered the stock certificates to a bank of the client's choice before payment was made. (These days your stock certificates – your physical shares – probably reside in the vaults of your brokerage firm or bank, but you can request to receive them for your own files.) Ordinarily for a DVP order the client had seven days to pay us. If the bank was out of town, though, we were given thirty days to collect the stock certificates and deliver them to the bank for payment. That meant the client had thirty days to authorize the bank to pay us.

Well, this client had picked a bank in Florida, so he had thirty days to watch the Eastern Airlines stock price surge up and down, which it did. It was enough to make anyone seasick. We rounded up the stock certificates and delivered them to the bank in Florida. Then really bad news about

Eastern Airlines came out and the stock crashed. The client told the bank to reject payment to us. He told them he had never ordered the stock.

And he was still within his thirty days so we had to eat the loss. Which meant, according to the Senior Manager, that I had to eat the loss. I was supposed to have known this client; I was supposed to have guessed that the guy would be unreliable, even though he had purchased plenty of stocks before and had always been a good client. The loss was going to come out of my commission.

"Wait a minute," I said to the Senior Manager. "I'm on a split commission with you. You take half of my earnings, you should split my error 50/50, too!"

We argued about that for a while, and then he agreed.

(The biggest secret to my career success is that I never caved if I felt I was right.)

It helped that my old friend, the walk-in, had been sitting by my desk visiting when the client had requested the order of Eastern Airlines. He vouched that the client had called me and asked for it – I had not recommended it – so I was not directly responsible for the fiasco. The company and I split the loss as we had agreed.

My favorite guest in the chair beside my desk, though, was Mildred. She lived with her husband in New Jersey. Their kids were nearly the same ages as Stephen and Victor, so with them in school, she had a little time on her hands. She'd come and sit with me for hours, chatting but also listening to me make phone calls to clients. I knew she was learning from me, though she wasn't thinking that way at all. After about a year I said to her, "Mildred, isn't it time you got your own desk?"

First she was stunned. Then she laughed.

The Hornblower training program was full that year, so she found another brokerage firm that had a training program, applied, and was admitted. Back when we were young girls, Mildred had once come into the kitchen wearing makeup. My father blew his top and ordered her into the bathroom to wash it off. "Young ladies should not look like fast women!" he said. Mildred took after my mother; she washed it off. Now, finally, my sister was doing for herself. And she loved it.

It was 1967 then, the same year that an interesting piece of news was circulating around Hornblower & Weeks, along with the rest of Wall Street: Muriel Siebert was applying to own a seat on the New York Stock Exchange.

In my four years in the financial industry, I had never heard of another "lady stockbroker." Now here was one who was so successful, she had just founded her own firm, Muriel Siebert & Co., Inc. There had certainly never been a woman who owned a seat on the Exchange, either. (Owning a seat allows you to trade on the floor of the Exchange, not just run orders through a market maker. It's prestigious and expensive; at that time the price of a seat was about half a million dollars.) The Board of Governors was reviewing her application, and with her track record it should have been a simple decision.

Well the Board gave her the run-around – I remembered how ridiculous they had been about allowing me onto the floor of the Exchange for my training program – but just before the end of the year, they came to their senses and sold her a seat. I had even more enthusiasm and drive after that, knowing that such a thing was possible.

The more enthusiasm I had, the bigger nuisance I was to the Analysts. The key to this business is information; you get that, you get the clients. All the brokers wanted to pick the Analysts' brains, but only a few of us took the time and care to relate to them as human beings. I enjoyed talking with them, not just the fruits of our conversations. The Analysts appreciated that about me.

One day they had a chance to show their appreciation. It was 10 a.m. I was moving to a new desk that day, which meant moving all of my possessions and a lot of bending down and standing up, so I was wearing a pantsuit. Under any other circumstances, slacks were not accepted at the workplace.

My phone rang. It was one of the Analysts.

"Norma, I made you a lunch appointment today at the 21 Club with Yura Arkus-Duntov, who used to be at The Dreyfus Fund. He just founded the Equity Growth Fund of America. He wants someone to convey our information to him but maybe you can service his portfolios!"

Well, I had to stay on the phone with that Analyst for a little while, just to get over my shock. This was the biggest thing that had happened for me since Harry Winston. The Dreyfus Fund was one of the most influential institutions on Wall Street, and the Equity Growth Fund was bound to be a big player, too. For the Analysts to recommend me to Yura Arkus-Duntov, this was tremendous. They had confidence that I might be able to impress him into becoming a client.

And I was wearing slacks. That was not good. Women did not wear pants to do business at that time.

When I got off the phone and the office heard that I had been selected to meet with Duntov, there was an uproar. My male counterparts still had the deep-lying assumption that a woman could not be at the top of a group full of men. Earl just stated to the room that the Analysts had picked me. That silenced them.

I ran, I did not walk, the two blocks to Saks Fifth Avenue. I had less than two hours to buy a suit and have it altered (everything had to be shortened for me), choose shoes, gloves, a hat, and get over to one of the swankiest restaurants in the city to meet the man with his finger on the pulse of the market. When I entered the 21 Club I dropped off my credit card with the maitre d', as I always did for business lunches. It prevented awkwardness when the check was dropped. I couldn't allow a client to pay for lunch, but etiquette required that the man reach for the tab.

"Well," said Yura Arkus-Duntov of The Dreyfus Fund and the Equity Growth Fund of America, "I've never been treated by a lady before!"

"Think of me as a colleague," I smiled.

My conversation with that tall, slight man was one of the best hours in my career. I had real confidence by then and could answer all his questions to his satisfaction. By the end of the meal, he was my client.

Not too long after that the U.S. went off the gold standard. The morning after the government's announcement, everyone thought that the market was going to open with a crash. Yura called me up early, named a stock issue, and told me to watch it closely. "Now it might not crash, Norma. But if it does, buy, buy, BUY!"

Everyone on Wall Street was nervous that day, except Yura. He sounded giddy and delighted. Ever since then, every time the stock market crashes, I hear Yura crowing in my ear, "Buy, buy, BUY!" And I do. His advice has never been wrong. When the rest of the investors are panicking, that is a savvy investor's playground!

1968 was definitely a year of wild swings. The '60s, of course, had been full of race riots, murders of civil rights activists, Vietnam protests, The Beatles and rock and roll, the space race, and growing attention for the women's movement. But 1968 was especially volatile. In April Martin Luther King, Jr. was shot and killed, the worst of tragedies. In the same month, a new Civil Rights law was passed. Going off the gold standard dizzied the stock market in March, yet in June the market reached a new record for trading volume: over 21 million shares traded in one day.

Personally, I had some steep peaks and valleys that year, too. I had enough confidence and knowledge now to look for bigger clients – institutions, pension plans, and such. And for the first time, I made $100,000 in commissions in one year. I had become one of the top brokers at Hornblower & Weeks in just five years. In recognition, I was invited to join the Advisory Board of the firm, an outstanding honor.

It made no impression on Sam at all.

By now we had almost completely stopped talking to each other. Mostly we tried not to be in the house at the same time, so that we wouldn't start fighting and upset the children. We didn't eat together. We didn't sit together. There were still the nights, though. We didn't have a spare bedroom so Sam and I were still sharing a room and a bed – but "sharing" is the wrong word. We were ghosts to each other. We moved around in silence, thinking about our own separate lives, not listening to each other, not looking at each other.

I had finally found a reliable housekeeper for Elysa, but the boys were not doing well in school. In May 1968 there was a strike by the teachers of New York City. As the summer dragged on it became clear to me that they weren't going to settle anything before the next school year started. So without consulting Sam – it wouldn't have been a conversation, it would have been a useless fight – I enrolled the boys in private schools. I could afford to do it without involving him. I chose the Peddie School in New Jersey for Victor, the Cheshire Academy in Connecticut for Stephen; different schools because they had very different personalities. They were fifteen months different in age and clashed a lot.

When I drove them to their new schools, they both cried, though they were approaching their teens. It wrenched me. I tried to explain, tried to be honest. "You may not love it at first but life will be easier here, I promise. There won't be your parents arguing. And this is better than housekeepers, right?"

They didn't buy it. They felt abandoned and there was nothing I could say to make them feel better. They had lost all their friends, everything that was familiar to them.

Maybe some parents could do this without guilt, but not me. I visited Doc Grossman as soon as I could.

"So it was necessary," he said. "You see that."

"Yes," I said.

"Does it solve the biggest problem?" he asked.

"No," I admitted. I could sleep in one of the boys' rooms now, but Elysa was still stuck in the house, trapped between Sam and me.

"You're going to ask for a divorce," Doc said.

"I can't, I can't," I said.

I had mentioned the possibility to my mother and I could still hear her moaning over the phone, "Oy oy oy, with three children, what are you going to do, nobody wants a woman with three children! A divorce in our family? No! It's a shame!"

It was more important what other people thought than how I felt.

But Doc Grossman spoke up and drowned out my mother's voice in my head. "Yes you can! You can, you can, you can!" he said.

And by the next year I could, and did.

Looking back on 1968, one September day stands out. It was just another adventurous day in the market at the time, but it became so much more.

That morning the phone woke me up at seven a.m.

"Norma?" a man called through the earpiece. "It's Larry!"

"Who?" I said.

He explained: Larry, my old neighbor across the street, the doctor who had moved with his family to Queens when construction was finished on their house.

"Norma, listen! There's a new stock coming out today, Elba Systems, my broker can't give me any new issue stock. Can you buy some shares for me?"

"OK, I don't know what my allotment is but I'll give you what I can."

An allotment was a number of shares of a new stock offering given to me, in anticipation of the company going public, that I could parcel out to my clients. (My clients would then have seven days to pay me for them.) The allotment was different for every new stock offering so I wouldn't know what this one was until I went into work.

Well, I went in to the office and I gave Larry all I could of Elba, 200 shares. Most allotments were usually "odd lots" – less than 100 shares. His Elba shares doubled their worth in the first two hours. The phone rang.

"That's enough, Norma!" Larry cried over the phone. "I've doubled my money, sell, sell, sell!"

"Larry, I can't sell them until you pay for them!"

So he drove as fast as he could from Queens to my office with a check.

Then I tried selling him some other shares, and he bought them. About two years later, when I was divorced and he was separated, we ran into each other at a wedding. That's when he asked me out for dinner. The rest isn't history; it's very much my present. We have been married for forty years.

The divorce from Sam – well, what can I say. It was ugly. It took a year of fighting to get him to agree to one. Then it took another year of lawyers and paperwork and more fighting to finalize it; New York doesn't make it easy on couples. All of this we did while still living our ghost lives in the same house. The day our lawyers called us to confirm that it was finalized I felt so scared, but also so very, very relieved. We had been together for almost twenty years and I had hung on for far too long. But I didn't have a choice – until I changed my mind and my life and gave myself the choice.

Then and Now

As I write this, the latest uproar in the presidential election race between Barack Obama and newly confirmed Republican candidate and millionaire Mitt Romney is actually about Romney's wife, Ann.

Ann Romney has been campaigning on her husband's behalf and Romney has been vocal about relying on her advice. In early April of 2012 he said to the American Society of News Editors,[2] "My wife... reports to me regularly that the issues women care about most is the economy and getting good jobs for their kids and for themselves." A week or so later, on CNN's TV show *AC360*, Hilary Rosen, a managing director at a political consulting firm, said that she thought it was wrong for Mitt Romney to use his wife as his guide to women's economic struggles when Ann Romney "had never worked a day in her life," referring to the fact that she had been a stay-at-home mother.[3]

Well, everybody started slinging rocks, claiming that Hilary Rosen had denigrated the difficult job of being a mother (despite the fact that she herself has two children). Look, you can't say that a woman is "only" a mother or "only" a homemaker. That's a great job and a hard job, and Rosen realized this and publicly apologized.

But there's another question being asked during all the ruckus: How much can a stay-at-home millionaire's wife know about the economy? Are her opinions on the economy valid?

My opinion is, Ann Romney didn't need to know how the economy works. With her husband's income, she could afford to stay at home, and she was a mother with a lot of help. A woman who has to work, whether or not she has children, you better believe that she knows how the economy works. She has to. A working woman is very aware of what's coming to her in terms of salary, health insurance, and other benefits, and very aware of what she's spending.

---

2   Madison, Lucy. "Amid perceived advantage, Obama touts pro-women message." CBS News, April 6, 2012. http://www.cbsnews.com/8301-503544_162-57410569-503544/amid-perceived-advantage-obama-touts-pro-women-message/. Accessed April 17, 2012.

3   Rosen, Hilary. "Ann Romney and working moms." The Blog, Huffington Post, April 11, 2012. http://www.huffingtonpost.com/hilary-rosen/ann-romney-women_b_1419480.html. Accessed April 17, 2012.

She knows what her tax rate is. She knows if it's going to decrease or increase. She knows what a home economy is because she has to keep a budget. She has to watch her money carefully and make decisions: Do I buy these shoes? Do I not buy these shoes? I started my career because I had to. I struggled with balancing home and work. I had a lot of ends to meet and I agonized over my household budget. And I knew the economy. I knew it because I lived it. The wife of a millionaire cannot have that perspective unless she researches other women's experiences and even then, that is no substitute for experiencing it yourself – for being forced by circumstance to make tough financial decisions.

CHAPTER SIX
My Nureyev

IN EARLY 1972, the south tower of the World Trade Center accepted its first tenants. Businesses had started moving into the north tower over a year before, but the opening of the south tower meant that the world's tallest buildings were now officially up and running.

"You know the real reason why they built the world's tallest buildings?" I said to Larry over dinner one evening. "They're trying to get above the pollution."

In stark contrast to those fresh new buildings, the rest of New York City was in bad shape. The air was noxious. The subway trains were filthy, dark, and prone to breaking down. Crime was rising; the parks weren't safe. Mayor Lindsay's approval ratings were plummeting. It seemed like someone was always on strike: transit workers, teachers, sanitation workers.

I was very attached to the city I was raised in. I remembered being in the Hornblower training program when the city announced the name of the architect for the World Trade Center; my career and the world's tallest buildings had grown up together. But at street-level, the garbage, rats, roaches, smog, heroin, guns – this was no longer the city I knew and loved.

"Would you ever live in California?" Larry said.

"What brought that up?" I asked, surprised. We were still dating at the time, and he hadn't mentioned California before.

"My sister Sheila lives there. I've always wanted to live there, too, but my ex-wife wouldn't leave New York. I can't take the cold here, I don't like anything that's happening to the city, when I visit my sister I don't want to come home. Would you think about moving?"

"Do you want me to seriously consider it?"

"I'm hoping you'll think about it."

Considering what Larry had faced about my life, I felt this was a small favor to ask. Only a few months before, Stephen's school had called to tell me Stephen was in the hospital. I knew he had been skipping school, going hiking with girls from a sister school; he even went to Woodstock. He had also been getting into drugs, and this time he had overdosed. They found him just in time.

Well, Larry went with me to the hospital. I had been afraid that this kind of news would cause him to break up with me, but here he was helping me, and my son, too. So, yes, I could at least consider the idea of moving to California.

But I had to make sure of one thing.

"Larry, my career is very important to me and I intend to continue it. I'm not going to move to California just to become a homemaker."

"Good!" Larry said. "That's not enough life for my wife. And that's what I love about you, Norma."

We smiled at each other. We had talked about it before but now we knew for sure: We were going to get married.

How different he was from Sam! And from the men I had dated before Larry. Many of them had thought my career was unimportant. Others had hesitated to approach me because I was strong, and not all men appreciate strong women. I had had no interest in getting remarried, actually. Not to that kind of husband.

But my career was a delight to Larry. He had always had great admiration for his mother, who was a very strong woman, and he liked to see that strength in me. "It drives me crazy," he said, "to see women earn advanced degrees, then settle down as wives and mothers before they even start careers, never doing anything with their educations, their knowledge – such a waste. But you're different."

We were both different. We had mutual respect for each other from the start; falling in love came afterwards. I felt so lucky after a long day of work to be able to share my victories and talk through my problems with him.

Although there weren't that many problems to talk over. As a member of Hornblower's Advisory Board and one of their most successful Account Executives, I was at the top of my game. I couldn't say I had punched through the "glass ceiling" because that term wasn't used for career women until the 1980s, but I had punched through many, many assumptions, perceptions, and biases. The issue of being a woman in the securities business was almost nonexistent. (Some of my relatives were still giving me guilt trips, especially after I married Larry. "Your husband can support you now, you don't need to work!" The fact that I liked to work, that it was part of my personality, was not respected; and the success I'd achieved in my career wasn't respected either.) Obstacles at Hornblower, though, were usually just comical, such as the "antiquing" incident several months before....

A conference was being held in Palm Beach for Hornblower's most successful stockbrokers. Our spouses were invited, too. Larry and I were only dating but he was on the invitation list; I made sure of that. A few weeks before the trip, I received a call from one of the event's planners.

"We are going over the schedule of activities for the conference in Palm Beach and, well, on Saturday while all of the Account Executives are attending the presentations about the stock exchange, we arranged for the spouses to visit the antiques stores around town. Do you, uh –"

I didn't let her finish; I just started laughing. The idea of Larry poking around antiques shops and cooing over ceramic flamingos and seashell soap holders with a crowd of wives was priceless. I couldn't wait to tell him about it. Larry, all those years of medical training you went through, all your years in practice, just so you can go antiquing with the wives! No way!

"That won't work," I finally managed to say over the phone.

"Well, that's kind of what we thought," said the planner. "Do, uh, you have any ideas?"

"Yes," I said. "I think he'd like to sit in on the presentations. I'm sure he would enjoy that."

And he did.

Now it was 1972 and I was looking across a dinner table at my future husband. I was at the very top of my game but, I admitted, that wasn't enough for me. Maybe I could improve the game? With Larry here and Sam gone, there was only one part of my life that was really not satisfying: New York City.

"Let's visit Sheila," I said to Larry. "Let me see what California is all about."

There is no bottom to the stock market. There's no top, either. The sky is not the limit. As you expand, so does your world.

All that warm, beautiful sun in southern California – New York could not match that. Larry ran into Dr. Richard Marks on that visit, too. Dr. Marks had been Chief Resident during Larry's residency in surgery; then he moved to California. He told Larry, "If you're serious, move out here and you and I will form a loose partnership. It'll either work out or it won't but at least you'll be here!"

So we made the choice. Larry asked Sheila to contact a real estate agent and look around for a house in the Encino-Sherman Oaks area, near the practice of Dr. Marks. A couple of months later we flew out there again. We had less than a day in Los Angeles before catching a plane to San Francisco where Larry would get his license to practice surgery in California.

Sheila's agent picked us up at the airport in L.A. and drove us around to a few houses but none of them were right. We headed back to the airport. On the way the agent stopped at a pay phone to check in with her office. When she came back to the car she told us that a house had just come onto the market that was more like what we were interested in. It was an entertainment home with plenty of room for parties, a swimming pool, the works. We had just enough time to take a look. We drove by, we stopped in, we saw this lovely ranch home with a wide open feeling, so expansive after New York – those big rooms made me want to dance through them. We gave the owners the asking price; we didn't even bother haggling and squabbling about it.

California! Breathing room! Sunshine! Fifteen minutes by car to the beach! We were so ready. I didn't want to come back to New York at all but, of course, a lot had to be done there. Including obtaining a marriage license, which we took care of as soon as possible. Larry – not just my husband, but my partner, too – I didn't think life could be so good. (Oddly enough, in 1972 I was the same age Margot Fonteyn had been when Nureyev came into her life and jumpstarted the second half of her career. Larry and California were my Nureyev...)

We immediately started packing for the Golden State. I had only one concern left about the move: How would Hornblower & Weeks react? Would they give me a transfer to their Beverly Hills office? The answer was not a given.

Of course I talked it out with Earl first, and of course he wanted to give me the transfer, but he didn't have the authority. So one afternoon he and I stepped into the office of the Senior Manager, the same man who had bought the Brooklyn Bridge from me almost a decade ago – but only after I made sure the price was fair.

After we exchanged pleasantries, I asked him a question that had been on my mind for a long time. "I've noticed that Hornblower never offers its female employees" (a few of them had joined me by now) "any of the management positions that open up in the firm's offices around the country. Can you tell me why that is?"

"Well," he said, and sat back. He looked like he was preparing just in case this was going to turn into a fight. "I'll tell you, Norma. We don't offer those management positions to women because women won't move to a different city. In a woman's life, her husband's career comes first. It's different for men. A man will move easily. He just picks up his wife and kids and goes. But a woman can't do that with her family."

He watched me carefully. Earl was watching me, too. I thought about his statement for a while.

"I guess you're right," I said. And the truth was, he *was* right. At that time, that was how families worked.

But how could I phrase my next question? I was worried that beneath the answer he just gave, maybe there were other, less acceptable reasons. I had not forgotten my colleague in the training program who had accused me of taking away a job opportunity from a man who needed and deserved it more. If I asked for a transfer, would the Senior Manager say something similar? Would he force me to either stay or quit the firm completely?

"What's on your mind, Norma?" he asked.

I decided to be aggressive about it. That had served me well so far in my career.

"I'm moving to California with my husband," I said, "and I'd like to be an Account Executive at the Hornblower Beverly Hills office."

"You mean you're not asking for a management position?" he said.

"No," I said.

"Why not?"

"Because I like what I do."

"Oh. Well. Of course we are very sorry to lose you, Norma, but yes, I think we can make that transfer happen. Let me call them."

He got on the phone right then and there to call the Beverly Hills office. While he was on hold he asked, "It's going to take you a while to put together a new book of West Coast clients. Can I offer you a salary and a draw against your commissions to tide you over?"

"Yes!" I said.

"And have you thought about your New York clients?" he asked. "What would you like to have happen with them?"

99

I couldn't believe he was asking. The usual practice was that the other Hornblower brokers would simply attack my book and divvy up my clients among themselves. Was there another way to handle my book?

"Well, since you asked," I said, "my sister Mildred just became a stockbroker. If Hornblower hired her –"

"If she is anything like you, we would be happy to." And right about then the Beverly Hills office came on the line and confirmed that my transfer was welcome.

I was amazed, and touched, that he had been so helpful, when I had been sitting there worrying. They really valued me. As it turned out, they did hire Mildred; and the salary and draw they gave me helped to keep my family afloat while Larry went through the difficulties of starting a new practice. The loose partnership didn't work out after all; two surgeons together don't make a good marriage. Larry started over again to build his own practice, working in emergency rooms, hosting dinner parties with me so that he could meet referring doctors – one step at a time.

Larry and I moved to California on April Fool's Day, which still makes me chuckle. It was the right, light-hearted, giddy day to start life in the bright sun.

We brought our families with us. Elysa, of course – transitioning to having a stepfather had been difficult for her even though she had known Larry before, when he was living across the street from us. I knew transitioning to a new state was a lot to ask of her, but eventually the sunshine and other advantages of California helped her settle a little bit.

Victor and Stephen were still in school, which I still felt guilty about. Wealthy people put their children in boarding schools all the time; somehow it never occurred to me that it was okay for me to do the same. The boys didn't seem to mind that they'd be flying to California on a regular basis, though.

Larry's parents also came out on the plane with us and moved into an apartment not far away from our home. A couple of years later my parents joined the California party, too.

But best of all, the year after Larry and Elysa and I settled into Encino, my sister and her husband moved to L.A., too. So my old book of clients was split up after all, but the most important thing was that my best friend wasn't a continent away from me anymore. I had called Mildred and David so many times, promoting California like I was an advertising agency. At last my campaign worked. David had just closed his business and he decided to seek new opportunities in California instead of New York.

I tried to convince my brothers to come, too, Harvey and Martin, but they both owned piece goods companies in New York's Garment District, so moving wasn't such a desirable prospect for them. Harvey actually came out to visit and check it out, but one of his first days there he came back to our house and walked in the door saying, "What a crazy state!"

"What's the matter?" I asked.

"I gotta wait on the corner for the light to change before I can cross! I don't have time for that. I can't make it in California, too slow for me!"

There were also two people who felt like family who I couldn't bring with us, either: Earl and Irma. Saying good-bye to Earl wrenched me terribly. If not for him, I wouldn't be where I am.

* * *

California businessmen weren't any more prepared for a woman in the financial industry than New York businessmen had been. The California version of the ideal woman was a Hollywood starlet, which I definitely was not. Although I was a strawberry blonde now, thanks to my hairdresser who convinced me that black hair was too New York. When I came home the first time with my new color, Larry said, "Who are you?!" But he loved it, I loved it; my life had brightened up in every way.

However, black hair, blonde hair, I was a woman, and in California women worked in real estate, not in the financial industry. When I talked to the California businessmen about securities, they usually gave me the feeling that I was wasting their time, like they wanted to pat me on the head like a cute little girl and send me on my way. I wanted to knock on their foreheads and say, "Hey, catch up to the East Coast, women have careers over there!" Here I was, pioneering – again.

Actually, in California almost everybody was working in real estate, and the West Coast businessmen were much more interested in that than in securities. The stock market was considered a secondary investment, so I had to break through that barrier too. I had to educate them about why securities were a good investment in the first place, before I could interest them in the specific offerings of my firm.

The time difference added brand new problems, too. The stock market in New York opened at 10 a.m. and closed at 3:30 p.m., 7 a.m. and 12:30 p.m. on Pacific time. My day started at 5 a.m. so as to get to the office with plenty of time before the opening bell.

"Oh, so you're only working half-days?"

I lost patience with that question pretty quickly. It seemed like everyone I knew asked it. I definitely was not working half-days. The California businessmen came into their offices at around 9 a.m., but that wasn't a good time to call because they just wanted to check their mail and make their appointments for golf or tennis in the afternoon. I had a window of time just before lunch when they'd talk business with me, and another one just after lunch. Then they had their afternoon golf and tennis appointments. I had one more window in the late after-noon before the end of the business day, but of course, by then the stock market had been closed for hours. My days were twelve hours long and at the end of them, I was exhausted. And of course, then I'd head for home to take on my other job as wife and mother.

All of the time that I wasn't on the phone I was doing research. Not just researching who I could cold call, but researching opportunities in the market. Oh, I missed my Analysts. I missed their expertise and their friendship. It's never as easy to connect on the phone.

I increased my time spent on research because I needed more opportunities to offer to potential clients. It was so difficult to get the attention of these West Coast business-men – and keep it – every day I needed a full array of exciting opportunities, not just good deals. Every time I heard "no," I needed to be able to tell them the story of another opportunity, just to keep them on the phone. And they said "no" more often than New York business-men did. It didn't help that cold visiting was much more difficult to do in this car culture. I had to rely more on referrals from my clients.

One of the best things I did, though, was keep track of every "no," very specifically. Each opportunity I offered that was turned down, I watched how it performed in the market. If it did well, I'd call any businessman who had said "no" to it and talk to him about it. "I just want to remind you that I suggested this to you, and this is how well it did. Now, you didn't buy that time, but if you give me five minutes now, I have another opportunity you could consider...."

I refused to give up, and I came up with very specific ways to keep trying. I had to think like a strategist and have three different ways to accomplish any single goal; that was the only way to assure I'd achieve it.

Gradually my approaches worked and many California clients were added to my book, but the process was wearing me out. The brightest hour for me every day was taking a late lunch with my sister after the stock market closed. Our favorite restaurant was the original Cheesecake Factory on Rodeo Drive. We would talk over every aspect of the financial industry, our lives, the world in general. One day I realized that my favorite part of my career was the breaks I was taking from it. How did that happen? That was unacceptable.

But what could I do?

Mildred had the answer this time. She was working at Bear Stearns and felt very comfortable there; her world had expanded. She had even changed her name to Nicole, which I agreed was much better suited for her petite, bubbly self. One of the things Nicole loved best at Bear Stearns was her relationship with the Analysts they had in their Los Angeles office. I had taught her well! Now she had with them what I used to have in New York. I didn't waste time being envious. I contacted her manager. He was impressed with my track record and hired me immediately.

But although I enjoyed working there, it was still the same game, and I was aching for some new challenges. Always a dancer, I had to keep moving. I started thinking, wondering, looking around....

And I identified one giant hole in the state of California's financial industry. From north to south, Crescent City to Tijuana, in 1973, there was not one money market mutual fund.

Money market mutual funds had existed in New York for a short period of time, and they served a specific purpose for brokerage firms and clients. They were places to park cash. If a client sold some stock and his brokerage firm had a money market mutual fund, his broker could transfer the proceeds of the sale into the fund instead of into a bank. The fund would invest the cash into U.S. Treasury bills or other government agency securities. When the client wanted to use his money to invest in stock or other products again, the fund would sell his shares to give him the cash to invest.

For clients, it was a safe holding place for their cash. They would earn a higher rate of interest than a savings account at a bank could produce, and the money market mutual fund was more convenient than undergoing multiple transactions between banks and the brokerage firm. It was also more convenient for the brokerage firm, and a way of staying on the client's radar. Instead of the cash disappearing out of sight, out of mind, into some bank, it was nearby in arm's reach, ready for the next investing opportunity.

They were tremendously useful and California didn't have a single one.

"Nicole," I said over lunch one day, "that's a big hole but we could fill it. What if we started our own money market mutual fund?"

A simple question – but with enormous import. We would be introducing something truly new to California. What an adventure!

My sister loved the idea. We proceeded to talk it over thoroughly with everyone whose opinion we respected, until one of my clients said, "You should talk to my friend, he's a lawyer who specializes in filing applications for new issues with the SEC."

That's how things happen, more often than not: you talk and talk, as if you're poking a stick around the bottom of a pond, determining its depth, until suddenly half the stick disappears and you've found the deep water.

The U.S. Securities and Exchange Commission (SEC) is the federal agency that regulates companies that are publicly traded. Any company, including money market mutual funds, that wants to go public and trade on the stock market has to apply to the SEC. The agency had a reputation for being tough but their reviews of applications usually took about three months, six months tops. The attorney had indeed filed applications many times to the SEC, and he was very excited when he heard our proposal. "Let's do it!" he cried.

Well, okay, it's one thing to express enthusiasm, it's another thing to sit down and get it done. But when we heard that the attorney had recruited a CPA who was also interested in the proposal, and that CPA had brought on some of his clients to be investors and board members, too, and they had already raised $100,000 – the minimum required by the SEC to start a money market mutual fund – well, Nicole and I quit our jobs.

Eventually the attorney, the CPA, and the CPA's clients raised a million dollars, the amount required by the SEC for the fund's first transaction. Meanwhile, Nicole and I arranged everything the application required, from identifying a custodian bank to recruiting brokerage firms to work with us, to finding the securities we'd be purchasing for the fund. It was a staggering amount of work, but we put together a wonderful package.

The hardest part was talking to banks and brokerage firms. They didn't know what a money market mutual fund was! Talk about selling an intangible – I felt like an alien speaking a different language. We talked to the banks first and manager after manager stared at us blankly.

"You're starting a what?" they'd ask. We would explain. "And you want us to what?" they'd ask. We would explain further. And more often than not, the next thing they'd say was, "Well, girls, you're competing with our business. So, no." They wouldn't hear the pitch and they certainly couldn't overlook the fact that we were women.

But we never stopped knocking on doors and explaining, and eventually we found a gentleman with vision at the First Pennsylvania Bank. They became our custodian bank, responsible for maintaining the clients' accounts. One task down.

Finding brokerage firms to work with us was not an easy task either, for the same reason. They didn't know what a money market mutual fund was and they didn't want to know. They were suspicious of anything new. With every ounce of patience we had, we explained over and over again to anyone who would listen why these funds were so useful for the brokerage firms. And we convinced enough of them to sign on: second task down.

Then there were the government securities – Treasury Bills and the like. Acquiring those for the fund was not as simple as calling up the government. We needed to come to some kind of arrangement with a bond house that bought securities from the government in round lots, which allowed the bond house to negotiate higher rates of interest. If we could buy our securities from a bond house, our clients could earn those same high rates of interest. That was one of the major advantages of a money market mutual fund.

However, we couldn't afford to purchase a round lot from a bond house. Only the biggest funds and brokerage firms could do that. We talked to dozens of bond houses, trying to figure out what we could do. Finally we found a trader at a bond trading firm who said, "You have a great idea here, come on, I'll help you out! I'll give you tail pieces, okay? When one of the big funds or firms only buys three-quarters of a Treasury lot, I'll sell you the other quarter." Another gentleman with vision! (The trader and I are still friends.) Third task down.

We named our fund "Liquidity Fund" and the attorney submitted the application. The waiting period began. Nicole and I finished our side of the process: renting office space and furniture, hiring employees, and a million and one other tasks to realize our business.

Three months passed. Nothing from the SEC. Well, okay, it was a small fund and Nicole and I had only been employed as brokers to date. Although our package was perfect and all of our board members were well regarded, we could understand a little bit of hesitation on the part of the SEC.

But more months passed, and now the SEC was responding to the attorney with questions. Not substantial questions about our application – stupid ones. They asked about and challenged and insisted on the pettiest of details. It got so ridiculous I said to Larry, "What's next, are they going to mark up our punctuation? Oh you've got a comma in the wrong place, we can't approve this!" The SEC nitpicked us month after month after month. Nicole and I were furious. Our application should have been a no-brainer and this was how they were treating it?

"To be honest," our attorney said, "I think they're messing you around because you're women."

The SEC didn't think these two women were for real. Or worse – the longer we stuck with the process, the more they didn't *want* us to be for real. They didn't want us to succeed.

Over a year after we submitted the application, the SEC approved it and gave us a date when we could open Liquidity Fund for business. The date they chose? December 26, 1974. The day after Christmas. Who opens a business on the day after Christmas?!

It was a slap in the face.

There was worse to come. During that year and a half, all those brokerage firms that Nicole and I had pitched the idea to – had hammered on their doors and talked ourselves hoarse until they grasped the concept and saw how amazing this opportunity was – well, they ran with the idea. They all started their own money market mutual funds, and the SEC was a hell of a lot more prompt in approving their applications. By the time we opened our business, we weren't the only money market mutual fund in California anymore, not by a long shot. We weren't new, we weren't exciting, and we were just a small operation. We weren't as attractive as all the other funds. We couldn't compete.

Soon the attorney, the CPA, and the other members of the board voted to close Liquidity Fund.

Nicole and I were heartbroken. Liquidity Fund was the first disappointment of my career, and it happened because we were women trying to make it in a man's world.

Then and Now

When Larry and I saw *The Iron Lady*, starring Meryl Streep as Margaret Thatcher, I cried. It was the moment when Margaret's future husband was proposing to her. She had stated that she was not going to give up her career to be a housewife; she couldn't die "washing up a teacup."

Denis Thatcher said to her, "That's why I want to marry you, my dear."

I looked at Larry and in the glow of the movie screen, I saw that he was crying, too. He had said much the same thing when he proposed to me.

We cried throughout the movie because it showed so much of what we had been through ourselves – the struggle to pay equal attention to career and family, the fight against narrow-minded men (and women), the odd, sometimes terrible, solitude of being Different. The movie recreated the famous photograph of Prime Minister Margaret Thatcher in bright blue, sitting with two rows of men in dark suits. I had a similar photo taken at the conference in Palm Beach for Hornblower's top earners: all men, plus me. I, too, "have done battle, every single day of my life."

I was sorry to hear that many young women today don't even recognize the name of Margaret Thatcher. That means that many of them probably have no idea just how difficult it was for her to attain the office of Prime Minister, how hard it was for women everywhere to break out of the cells we'd been shut in. I differ politically from Margaret Thatcher, but I empathize with and respect her mission, her career, her guts, and her willpower.

CHAPTER SEVEN
Bullies and Decisions

AFTER THEY SHUTTERED Liquidity Fund, Nicole and I went back to being stockbrokers. She went to Morgan Stanley and I went to Drexel Burnham; we could still have lunch together after the stock market closed, but not quite as often. However, Drexel Burnham was the most prestigious firm I'd ever worked for. By now I had enough clients that I could work more by referral than by cold calling. When I contacted a prospective client, I had not only the recommendation of a mutual colleague, but Drexel's impressive reputation, too. As soon as I named the firm, the California businessmen took notice. I didn't have to fight to keep their attention anymore. My career soared.

But deep down, I wondered if the SEC had broken me. Would I ever try anything new again? Of course every cold call, every new client, every shift in the stock market, was a small adventure. That's why I loved the business. But the big adventures – I didn't know if I had it in me. I didn't worry about it very often; it was just a thought that hit me some-times when I was in the car or reading in the bathroom.

There was a fight on another front that I needed to devote my attention and strength to anyway: Larry's custody suit for his children.

His kids had first come to visit us in California the summer of 1972. (Larry had converted his visitation rights from all the weekends in a year to the three months of summer.) Sheri was about to turn twelve years old and Tod was nine. Elysa fit right between them in age and although at first it was difficult for her not to be the only child in the house, soon they were all friends. The five of us had such a wonderful summer that at the end of it, Sheri and Tod begged not to go back to New York. They were distraught in the car to the airport. At the gate they cried, we cried, it was awful.

We knew that their home life in New York was making them miserable. Tensions ran high in the family. Their mother, Judy, was furious at Larry and badmouthed him to the children. The kids were home alone all the time and their needs were not being attended to. I know it isn't easy when there is a divorce, but Judy was making choices that I didn't agree with and didn't respect. Still, the custody agreement meant the children had to go back, much as we wanted them to stay.

They came to visit again the summer of 1973 and it was the same story: an idyllic three months and everyone in tears at the end of it, Sheri and Tod's last grief-stricken looks at us as they walked down the corridor to the plane.

A few months later, just past Christmas, our phone rang. It was Judy. "Where are Sheri and Tod? Do you have them? I know you have them, you kidnapped them!"

What?! "No, my god, what are you talking about, are they missing?"

Larry and I were beside ourselves. After Judy hung up on us, we started calling everyone we could think of who might know where the kids were. We knew they had been unhappy but Sheri had too much sense to run away, we thought. We hoped! But if not that, then maybe an accident had happened, or worse. No parent wants to start calling hospitals, looking for their children. It was a nightmare.

At nearly midnight, our doorbell rang. We opened the door and Sheri and Tod were standing outside, bags in their hands.

How on earth?!

"I saved my babysitting money and bought us tickets," Sheri said.

She was thirteen years old; Tod was ten.

The full story was that Sheri had started planning this when they flew home the previous summer. To her income from babysitting and money she saved from her Bat Mitzvah gifts, she added contributions from relatives – not telling them what it was for, but promising to pay them back. She arranged for someone (we didn't ask too many questions) to buy the one-way plane tickets. She decided how she and her brother should pack, keeping in mind that they didn't intend to ever go home again – what they took would be what they kept. She paid for a taxi to the airport in New York, somehow talked the airline into letting them board despite the rule that minors had to be accompanied by an adult, and paid for another taxi to our house. They came all the way to our front door because they were afraid we would make them fly back.

I hadn't even known that Sheri was babysitting. This was – well, this was astonishing. She decided what she wanted, she strategized to accomplish it, then she boldly carried out the plan. And she took care of her little brother the whole time. We were flabbergasted.

Judy was enraged. Understandably – but she refused to believe that the children had done this all on their own. She kept accusing Larry and me of kidnapping them. A couple weeks later she arrived in California herself, bearing a court order mandating the return of the children to her. We were to deliver them to her lawyer's office in Century City. Our lawyer's office was there, too; Century City was a big commercial complex with a mall and many business offices.

We contacted our lawyer first, of course. He said first of all, there was an airline regulation stating that no one could be forced onto a plane if they didn't want to go. We were jubilant when we heard that. No matter what, Sheri and Tod could not be forced to board a plane to go back to New York. Our lawyer also said that Larry and I needed to give Judy every opportunity to take the children, so that it would be clear, when Sheri and Tod refused to go, that that was their decision and not ours. We all understood that, so when it came time to bring the children to Judy's lawyer's office, we did.

Our lawyer's office was located in one tower of the Century City complex; Judy's lawyer was located in a different tower. We brought the children and met Judy and her lawyer in the mall area that lay between the towers, and Judy walked Sheri and Tod away toward a bank of elevators. None of us were upset, even the children, since we had that airline regulation to rely on. All they had to say was, "Mom, we don't want to go with you."

Larry and I took a different set of elevators to our lawyer's office, sat in the reception area, and waited for a phone call from Judy's lawyer. And waited. And waited. Then one of us happened to look down through the interior window in the reception area. The window had a view of the mall, and there we saw Judy and a sheriff dragging Sheri and Tod away in handcuffs.

Handcuffs! Our kids!

We could see strangers around the mall staring at Sheri and Tod, pointing them out to their children, and I'm sure, making comments. It was humiliating and so unfair.

Our lawyer called Judy's lawyer. Apparently when Sheri and Tod continued to resist going back to New York, no matter what Judy said, she was so upset that she told the sheriff, "They're incorrigible!" That's a legal term in California, and it meant that the sheriff now had Judy's permission to put the children in steel handcuffs and escort them to the police station. From there they would be sent to Juvenile Hall.

Larry and our lawyer left immediately for the police station. By the time they arrived, Judy had given up and left the children alone there. But the police weren't allowed to hand Sheri and Tod over to Larry. By law they had to send the children to Juvenile Hall. So Larry and our lawyer followed the police car and arrived five minutes after they did. The children were already being processed.

Our lawyer introduced Larry as one of the children's parents. "He can take the children," he said. He figured it was worth a shot.

"Thank goodness!" said the Juvenile Hall official. "We're full and we have nowhere to put them. You're a parent? You take them!"

So when Larry came home that night, Sheri and Tod were with him. And here they stayed.

We were so grateful. Seeing the desperation leave Sheri and Tod's faces, happiness coming in to replace it, that made the whole custody battle worth it. The legal fight took over three years. Because Larry hadn't returned the children to Judy, he was held in contempt of court; if he set foot in New York, he would be arrested. Judy wouldn't speak to any of us, including her children, so every conversation had to be conducted through lawyers. The legal bills ballooned. Larry was also paying child support (and alimony) even though the children were living with him. He didn't want to trip any more legal traps by refusing to pay.

Fathers did not get equal consideration in custody cases in those days. (Neither did the preferences of the children.) Larry's only chance was to get Judy to agree to a settlement. In 1977 she finally did, probably because Sheri was almost eighteen. Larry had to borrow money from his Uncle Harry and Aunt Ida to pay Judy what was basically a lifetime alimony. (We worked very hard to pay them back, and we did.)

During all those years of constant bad news from our lawyers, there was one thing in particular that kept our spirits up: a certain look on Sheri's face whenever the topic was mentioned. It wasn't anger or fear; it was decisiveness, pure and simple. She had made her choice and she would not be bullied out of it. She was not going back.

* * *

A few years later, I felt that same look on my face. I didn't have to look in a mirror to know what it was.

By 1980 there was a new bully in my life, but I had no way of fighting back against this one. Nicole had been experiencing frequent headaches, some of them severe enough to prevent her from going into the office. Her doctor told her, "It's your nerves, you're working too hard."

Then she started bleeding. At first she thought it was just heavy periods, maybe early onset of menopause. But when it continued and she had it checked out, her gynecologist said she wasn't bleeding from her uterus. By this time the bleeding had intensified into hemorrhaging. The gyn sent her to a nephrologist, who suspected a problem. Nicole went in for surgery and came out minus a kidney. The doctor had found cancer so he removed the whole organ. He thought he had gotten all of the cancer, but we soon discovered that it was malignant.

It wasn't fair. I thought that a thousand times as I watched Nicole try every possible cure available. She was only forty-nine! But all I could do was visit her, hold her hand, try to keep her spirits up. The only people who could fight this bully were Nicole's oncologist and Nicole herself.

I was so afraid of being helpless but I knew, my fear was nothing compared to Nicole's. I resolved to be as strong as I could for her.

Then a second bully showed up.

Quite a few things had changed on Wall Street by 1980. The trading hours had been extended. Digitization was beginning and transactions were speeding up. On a single day in 1979 over eighty million shares had been traded; when I was a trainee at Hornblower the record was four million. International transactions were increasing across the board. Foreign brokers and dealers could be members of the New York Stock Exchange now, and diplomatic relations had been established with China – that had been unthinkable not too long before. Drexel Burnham was now Drexel Burnham Lambert. And Michael Milken, who had joined Drexel right out of business school long before I was hired, was staggering everyone on Wall Street with his department's wild successes. Hardly anyone understood how he was doing it.

I was still with Drexel (not in Milken's department). I had become good friends with another female stockbroker in my office – an Asian woman who brought in a lot of business from Hong Kong – and it was a pleasure working for such a highly respected firm. Just the name would bring me clients. One night Larry invited a friend and colleague to dinner. He was the administrator of Northridge Hospital, where Larry was working. During our chitchat I mentioned Drexel and the administrator raised his eyebrows.

"You're with a good firm," he said. "Would they be interested in looking into something for me?"

"What would you like?"

"I'm interested in acquiring Tarzana Hospital. They're a for-profit hospital and Northridge is a nonprofit, so I believe there would be significant tax savings if we bought them. Maybe enough to cover the purchase price?"

Why not? I agreed to present it to Drexel's corporate finance department. Well, they thought it was a great idea (and I am understating that). They called the mergers and acquisitions department in New York and they also thought it was a great idea (I'm still understating). The deal was becoming real, I was excited! Women never had the opportunity to broker this kind of a high-level transaction; the recognition and prestige would be considerable. This was the biggest single opportunity to come my way since I looked around and noticed that California didn't have any money market mutual funds.

Only one thing had to occur before we could officially make the offer to Tarzana Hospital. The Drexel mergers and acquisitions department had to send representatives from their bond department to California to review the financials of both hospitals. They had to determine whether the transaction was "doable."

So three men flew in, went over the books for a few days, and flew back to New York to report that the transaction was "very doable." (I don't have a monopoly on understatement.) The deal was a GO!

I admit, I danced around my house. But then, I did that all the time anyway. Larry and I hugged and then I called Nicole. Even though her voice was a little weak, she cheered! I told her I was dancing around and she laughed; she'd been watching me do that all her life.

I felt like pirouetting into the office the next day, too. Then I got a call from our corporate finance department. The deal was off.

Apparently one of the top executives in the mergers and acquisitions department had heard about the deal. He was a very powerful man and still is today – let's call him Mr. Manhattan. Well, Mr. Manhattan blew his top. "Who does that California girl think she is?" he said, about me. "My client's company owns Tarzana! I think I've got something to say about this!"

He didn't have to say much. He just killed the deal, because it wasn't his. (Soon after, Tarzana was sold to another hospital group, AMI.)

I ended the call with the corporate finance department and hung up the phone. Then I sat at my desk, absolutely still for once in my life. It was so unfair. I had been bullied out of the way and there wasn't a thing I could do about it. Just when I needed to be strong for Nicole this man had knocked me to the ground. I felt so helpless, so weak, so furious.

But I was having another reaction, too. I made myself ignore my other feelings and pay attention to this one. That was the moment I felt myself wearing the same expression I'd seen on Sheri's face: decisiveness.

I was not going to take this. I could not advance in a company where this kind of thing could happen. I had to do for myself.

So I decided to quit Drexel. I was going to be my own boss.

There was only one way to be your own boss when you were a broker: I had to start my own brokerage firm. That was going to be a very, very big adventure. All those years I had secretly wondered if I still had it in me – well, the answer was going to have to be, "Yes. I have it. I can do it. I must do it."

Then and Now

Nicole and I were so naïve, I see that now. We didn't need the backing of all those banks and brokerage firms to submit our application for Liquidity Fund to the SEC. All we needed was our well-respected attorney, our successful CPA and the money he raised, and our custodian bank, First Pennsylvania Bank. When we knocked on all those doors and told the banks and brokerage firms about the fund we were starting, being able to count them as future clients did help us get more individual clients to feel comfortable investing in our fund. But we'd already had enough clients to make a good start. And by telling those firms about our idea, we basically fed our baby to the competition. Once they understood the concept of a money market mutual fund, they liked it and went about forming their own funds. If we hadn't been so green, we would have waited until after we opened our doors to tell everyone about Liquidity Fund.

Naivety isn't always a curse, though. I think a certain amount of naivety allowed me to start my own brokerage firm. If I had really known what I was getting into, I might have felt too intimidated to start. So I can't judge those two bright, hopeful girls that we were too harshly. We made a mistake in business, but our spirits were just right.

CHAPTER EIGHT
On My Own

ONE NIGHT IN 1981 I was over at Nicole's house, watching TV. That had never been usual for us; we had always had too much to talk about to spend our time on TV. The cancer and the chemo were sapping Nicole's strength, though. She was so thin, had so little color in her face. Her natural bubbliness only surfaced when I could get her to laugh.

She was especially exhausted that day, stretched out on the couch while I was half-asleep in an armchair. I was tired out from all the work I'd been doing to start my brokerage firm. The TV shows and the ads were all running together in a stream of sound and color. In one of my more awake moments I noticed an ad with Dick Cavett, a famous comedian who had a talk show on PBS. In the ad he was sitting next to a blond woman named Jill — a homemaker, he called her, and she confirmed it. He asked about her Apple personal computer that was sitting on a desk between them. It was one of the ugliest things I'd ever seen, a hunk of beige and black plastic. It looked like a shoebox for giant orthopedic shoes. But a brightly colored bar graph was building itself on the computer's screen; that was interesting.

Dick asked if Jill was using the computer for household budgeting. She replied, "Actually I'm working in gold futures," and tapped on the keyboard. Dick was surprised. For the rest of the ad he kept trying to talk about households and she kept talking business. The last thing she said was that she owned a small steel mill. Dick looked profoundly uncomfortable. Jill glanced at the camera and I laughed out loud, because her look clearly said, "This guy's an idiot."

"That's me!" I exclaimed, "That's my life, that's me!" I was laughing, Nicole was laughing; we couldn't believe how perfect it was. I had just purchased an Apple computer in order to get stock quotes. Renting one of the stock quote machines that had replaced stock tickers and boards would have come at a staggering cost. I had worried about that for months. Overhead was not my friend! The big brokerage firms could handle hefty expenses, but for my company, it was just me and my savings.

But in 1980 I had seen a different ad for Apple computers. I hadn't known whether you could get stock quotes through a computer but I called Apple to ask, and they directed me to a company that did, in fact, provide that service. I called Apple right back and ordered an Apple II. Even the Apple representative was impressed. Very few people outside of the military and universities were using network services at that time; the World Wide Web wouldn't be invented until nearly a decade later. Once again I was a pioneer.

The cost of starting my firm was also the reason why I didn't officially quit Drexel until 1981. I needed to buy time to put my brokerage firm together, as well as a safety net in case my application wasn't approved. As I continued to service my clients' portfolios, I did the work of starting my firm on the side. Strictly speaking, that was taboo, but I had experienced how Drexel treated loyal employees; they scuttled their deals.

I first began the process of registering my brokerage firm, Yaeger Securities, by contacting the National Association of Securities Dealers (NASD), who would review my application. They were also going to function as my supervisor for the life of the firm, so they had a big job to do. They assigned a representative to monitor my application process to make sure I arranged everything correctly, and of course I found a lawyer with experience in these applications to counsel me as well.

For once in my life, I didn't have to deal with a representative being surprised that I was a woman. Although the only other woman I knew of who had started her own brokerage firm was Muriel Siebert, I now had nearly twenty years of professional experience and the NASD representative respected that. However, he was baffled by *why* I would want to do this. I had a great job with a prestigious firm and I would be stepping down into the smallest of companies – just one person. I told him my story about Tarzana Hospital and that cleared up his confusion.

The most important step of starting Yaeger Securities was making sure that it could function financially. As one of the smallest brokerage firms that the NASD would register, Yaeger Securities had a minimum capital requirement of $5,000 at all times, over and above expenses. I put up the initial $5,000 from my own money. But I also needed capital to transact trades that would hopefully run up to millions of dollars. Major firms have their own clearing back offices for this, but that wasn't an option for me. So I signed an agreement with Pershing & Company, whose sole business was clearing transactions for small firms. They would handle the trades, send confirmations to my clients, and hold my clients' cash. Without them, I wouldn't have had a company.

Pershing didn't provide Analysts, but I had done quite a bit of research analysis myself since I moved to California. I could also rely on Analysts I had been working with for years.

I took tests for two new licenses: the principal's license to show that I could supervise an entire firm, and the financial principal's license to demonstrate that I could satisfy the NASD's heavy financial reporting requirements – they were going to audit my firm every month. Those tests reminded me of how much I owed to the Hornblower & Weeks training program. Because I had been trained in every department of a brokerage firm, I knew how to set up and run a whole firm. They hadn't limited me by only teaching me what I "needed" to know.

Then there were the hundreds of other things to do: rent office space, make sure the plaque on my office door satisfied NASD requirements, register with the Securities Investor Protection Corporation (SIPC) and send them my first dues, arrange for telephone and other utility services, organize all the filing and technological systems, learn how to use my new Apple computer and how to network to the stock quotes company (there were no commercial internet service providers at the time, so that wasn't easy), and on and on. I took a wild leap into the future and landed in paperwork and minutiae, but that's usually how it goes. It took a little of the shine off the achievement, but the steady, methodical work also kept me from being terrified. I would celebrate the achievement later, after the firm was up and running.

Doing all the tasks would have been more fun if Nicole could have split the work with me as we did when we started Liquidity Fund, but sometimes she was too sick to even discuss details and offer suggestions. I was constantly torn as I worked on Yaeger Securities, wanting to spend more time with my sister. There were nights when I came home, put my head on Larry's shoulder, and just cried.

It became clear to me that Yaeger Securities couldn't be a one-person operation; there would be too much work and I would be too lonely. I had rented an office from a company that provided office space, utilities, and a pool of secretaries for a number of small companies, but I also needed an assistant. She would help with the monthly NASD audits, answer the phones, and do a thousand other things in the normal course of servicing clients' portfolios. And maybe she could provide a little friendly atmosphere, too.

I placed an ad in the papers and started interviewing applicants but I wasn't overly impressed with anyone. There were still plenty of secretaries who resented working for a woman, and I was not easy to work for. I was still a tough boss; that hadn't changed since my days at Hornblower & Weeks when none of the secretaries wanted to work for me. I wanted perfection and I wanted my assistants to think for themselves. They had to be sharp.

I was beginning to think that no one was going to meet my high standards. One afternoon an applicant for the job sat down in front of me. The first thing she said was, "I don't have years of experience because I've been a homemaker. But please hire me because I need to get some experience. I think we can work together, please just try me out, I will do my best."

Well, that was not the way job applicants began their interviews, not then and not now. But I had not forgotten that once upon a time I had been a homemaker starting out in a new career, too. When I interviewed Shirley Young I was impressed with the way she listened, thought, and made decisions and suggestions. I did hire her and she was a wonderful assistant, just as she had promised. We are still friendly today and she was invaluable to Yaeger Securities.

My parents and other relatives, by the way, still thought I was crazy for working at all. Thank god Larry was there with his enthusiasm and faith in me. Starting the firm was a bigger undertaking than I had thought when I embarked on it, but Larry wouldn't let me give up. "Go to it!" he'd say, any time I was wavering.

Last but not least, I needed clients. I knew Drexel would attack my book as soon as I quit, so before I notified the firm I was leaving, I talked to all of my clients, one by one, to invite them to transfer their accounts to my new brokerage firm. Yes, it would be a tiny firm, but Pershing & Company was known and respected for its clearing services, and most of these clients had been working with me for years. A few couldn't face leaving a large firm, but I was proud and pleased to see how many – almost all of them – transferred their accounts to Yaeger Securities (even when Drexel did, in fact, attack my book).

I don't think the NASD expected my firm to ever open, but eventually their representative performed his last task: he inspected my new office to make sure that all was in order. He was especially impressed with my Apple; he hadn't known stock quotes were available by computer yet.

A few days after the representative's visit to my office, he called to say that the NASD had accepted my application. That was a day for celebration! And the first morning I opened my office door, looking at the brass plaque with "Yaeger Securities" and "Member of SIPC," I felt such pride.

But my favorite moment from that day in 1981 might be when I dialed up for my first stock quote. I typed instructions into my Apple to contact the stock quote company in

New York, my computer rang like a phone, and then I was connected. No one got on and said hello. I just tapped the keyboard and wow, there it was, only a few glowing green numbers but incredibly important information, literally at my fingertips. And the stock quote happened so fast – no waiting on a party line for someone to answer my request, no hanging up and waiting half an hour for someone to call me back. I hadn't even had to wait for the computer to connect with New York. So few people were using computers to check stock quotes that I hardly ever got a busy signal those first couple of months.

I was still marveling at the stock quote when my phone rang. I looked up from my computer screen and when I picked up the phone, one of my clients said hello. Suddenly I remembered sitting at my desk at Hornblower on my first day as the Hat and Brooch Lady, back when I needed to display confidence and experience that I didn't yet have. I had persevered and I had excelled for twenty years, and now I was fully in control of my career. I was independent.

But my celebration of this achievement, which I had put off for so long, crashed abruptly, horribly. In June of 1982, Nicole died.

I was – devastated doesn't describe it. She was my sister in heart and soul as well as by blood. She was my best friend for so long and my sole support through so many difficult times.

I was no longer myself. She was gone and some of me had gone away with her. That sentiment is almost cliché but it is true; you are not fully yourself without your loved ones.

Thirty years later I still miss her. The loss of her still hurts.

* * *

After Nicole's death I shut down emotionally. I put my head down and worked – just worked, all the time. When I was working I didn't have to feel. They were dark days.

The work got done. Not only did the work get done, it got noticed. Brokers started calling to ask me if I would hire them. They wanted to get out of the big firms, too; they didn't like meeting quotas for sales and they wanted to be more independent. Yaeger Securities grew faster than I had imagined possible. I was working twelve-hour days again. Market hours were for servicing accounts; my after-hours were for managing the firm. I had to move the office for more space. I also bought one of the first fax machines, a Burroughs that was literally the size of a table.

As the firm grew, so did my capital requirements. The NASD had different requirements for different kinds of trades, for both my firm and the clearing company. It was only $5,000 to start Yaeger Securities, but to trade bonds we had a minimum capital requirement of $25,000. We outgrew Pershing & Company; they didn't have enough capital to clear big institutional deals. I wanted to switch us over to Merrill Lynch (specifically Broadcort Capital Corporation, one of their subsidiaries) but they had never heard of Yaeger Securities and weren't used to working with California firms. I had to fly to New York to speak to the principals of their clearing department. They examined our NASD records to make sure we were doing enough business to merit their involvement. We passed that test and they became our clearing company.

The growth of Yaeger Securities attracted other opportunities for me, too. An accountant I knew and several of his clients were raising money to start the Wilshire Savings and Loan Association, which would invest depositors' funds and make loans such as mortgages. It would be similar to a bank but regulated by a different institution within the government – the Federal Savings and Loan Insurance Corporation (FSLIC). They asked me if I'd like to be a start-up investor. Since Savings and Loans were doing quite well in 1984, I accepted their invitation.

Initial investors also served three-year terms on the Board of Directors of the Savings & Loan. The bulk of my work as a director was deciding how to invest the firm's capital to match the durations of their mortgages. I decided I wanted to make the safest investments possible. You can't get much safer than U.S. Treasury bonds, so that's what I chose. My three-year term flew by uneventfully.

Meanwhile, at Yaeger Securities I had so much work to do that I needed to create a management team. The monthly audits were so complex that I hired a Financial Officer. I hired a Sales Manager, too, which I hadn't thought I needed, but he impressed me. Like my brokers, he had found me and asked for a meeting. His specific pitch was limited partnerships.

"I don't do much with those," I told him, "My clients don't invest in them."

"Well, Norma, you're missing a good part of the business! I've been doing limited partnership transactions for a while and I have a lot of clients who are interested in investing in them. Bring me on, I'll bring my clients, I'll grow your business for you."

I called the firm where he'd been working, of course, and they gave him a positive report, so I added him to Yaeger Securities. I still didn't add limited partnerships to my clients' portfolios; I was confident in the same investment strategies I'd been using for years. His clients certainly seemed happy, though. His transactions were bringing in quite a lot of business.

With my expanded team we were able to service larger and larger clients and break into the international market, working with money managing firms who handled clients in England, Germany, and Japan.

But even with all of this growth and success, I was still grief-stricken and depressed. I missed Nicole so much.

Then I had the opportunity to bring another family member into the financial industry. My son Stephen had finished college and won a Rotary Club scholarship that sent him to Africa to study. He became fluent in French there, so when he finished his scholarship year, he moved to France to work. About a year later he returned to the United States and found a job in the mailroom of a New York advertising agency. He was planning to work his way up – a very traditional way of climbing a career ladder. The economy slowed down, though, and the agency had to do a layoff. Last ones in, first ones out, is the usual guiding principle in those situations, so Stephen was let go.

It was impossible to find a job at that time. All of my other children were in school: Victor was earning his Ph.D. in psychology and Sheri was earning a master's in business administration, specializing in healthcare, at the University of Miami. Elysa and Tod were both in college, studying marketing and psychology, respectively. Stephen was really my only child who had showed interest in the financial industry, and I thought he would have aptitude for it. I said to him, "Look, come into Yaeger Securities, get yourself a license so you have something to hang your hat on, sit at my trading desk and learn a little about the business. That'll keep you going until a job in advertising opens up."

He thought that was a great idea. I set him up with a school to prepare him for the test for his license, which he had no trouble passing; he had always been very bright. I arranged for him to sit next to my trader, which brought up fond memories of Nicole sitting by my desk at Hornblower & Weeks. Also, to welcome Stephen and to help him feel that he was really part of Yaeger Securities, Larry and I decided to give him some of the company's stock. Ownership would give him a sense of responsibility and maybe spur some ambition for the financial industry, too.

Stephen fit in well at the company. He was very personable, everyone liked him, and eventually he proved to be a great salesman. He brought in several nice accounts and he was especially skilled with bond trading. However, beneath his charm there was a substantial amount of anger that would snap out at unexpected moments. He was also taking advantage of the fact that he was the boss's son. Everyone else showed up well before seven a.m., which was when the market opened, but Stephen would saunter in at ten o'clock every day. During those three hours he was skipping – it reminded me of him skipping classes in high school – other people were having to do his work. His behavior continued for months and it affected other people's attitudes in the office. My brokers didn't hesitate to push back at me for what they perceived to be unfair treatment. The whole situation was unacceptable.

First I mentioned the problem to Stephen. He ignored me. Then I warned him. He continued to ignore me. After almost a year of this, I had to say, "Stephen, either you come in earlier or I'm going to let you go!"

It was one of the most difficult things I'd ever done. The guilt was overwhelming. Two decades earlier I'd had to leave him, in tears, at a private school; now I had to threaten to fire my own son?

Worse was coming. When I said that to Stephen, he almost sneered. "Well," he said, "if you're going to let me go, you have to buy back my stock."

131

So he would gain not only the interest that the stock had already earned, but also the worth of the stock, which was substantial and which he was not, by contract, entitled to after working there less than a year.

One of the principles I lived by in my career was to never cave. But this was personal. This was my son. It was bad enough that I was firing him; I was hoping that somehow we could smooth out the situation so that there wouldn't be tension between us. I agreed to his demand. We arranged a monthly payment schedule out of my pocket into his. And still, when he left the office for the last time, we were not on speaking terms. I felt that I had lost another family member.

* * *

Nicole's death had darkened my days at Yaeger Securities. The disaster with Stephen drove me into deeper depression. I was functioning, but only functioning; I didn't have any great feeling of thriving.

Yaeger Securities was certainly thriving, though. We worked our way up to a minimum capital requirement of $100,000, and we were doing the multimillion-dollar trades that I had hoped for.

Stephen was also thriving. I heard through our mutual acquaintances that he had gone to work for Michael Milken's high-yield bond trading department at Drexel Burnham Lambert. Stephen was living in Hollywood, going into work at six every morning, and making a killing at bond trading and sales. Maybe my firing him had been the best thing for him. I was still terribly sad that we were estranged, but I was very proud of his current success. I hoped that soon he would come around and we could heal our rift.

Society was thriving and expanding, especially in the area of gender equality. Margaret Thatcher was elected and re-elected Prime Minister of the U.K. In 1981 Sandra Day O'Connor was the first woman to be nominated to the U.S. Supreme Court. In 1983 Sally Ride was the first woman to rocket into space. And in 1986 Oprah Winfrey aired her first episode of *The Oprah Winfrey Show*.

The stock market was growing and thriving, too. In January of 1987 the Dow Jones Industrial Average, which is an index of the stock performances of thirty blue-chip companies, closed at over 2,000 for the first time. In July it closed above 2,500. By August it had almost doubled its points from its performance the previous year.

Oh, it's so easy to look back with hindsight and say that that growth was obviously too high, too fast, unsustainable. But when you know the stock market, you don't really need hindsight. A surprisingly rapid rise in the market usually does result in some kind of fall. The trick is to anticipate *when* the fall is coming. That's basically a guessing game, though, and I was no better at it than anyone else.

The descent began in early October. For a couple of weeks the ride was choppy, just enough ups to keep people in the market, but enough downs to get them scared. Really scared.

On Monday, October 19, one of my brokers sat down with a stock quote machine. (We had grown enough to afford several of them.) He entered a company's stock symbol and waited for a quote. He didn't get one. He just got a blank. We fiddled with the machine a bit, thinking the problem was us. Then we turned on the TV in the office and saw the news coverage of the market taking the biggest dive it had ever experienced. (For perspective, the crash on October 15, 2008 was a drop of 7.9%. On Black Monday in 1987, it dropped 22.6%.)

My brokers were going crazy. Shirley was going crazy. Larry was calling me and going crazy. Everyone was panicking. One of our friends who owned his own brokerage firm lost his entire net worth before he could even get an order off. He had been investing in a lot of smaller stocks and options and those companies just disappeared.

I was literally clinging to the arms of my chair as I watched the avalanche. I wanted to sit under my desk. There was nothing I could do. We couldn't get quotes so we couldn't put in orders. Nobody was picking up the telephone so we couldn't get information other than what we saw on TV. The more we watched the news – and we watched all day – the more we wanted to sell. All of us were dying to jump out of the market, but we couldn't.

That turned out to be a good thing. If we had had the ability to sell we might have made some scared stupid decisions. As it was, I had time to think about the big picture. I knew that the stocks we had recommended for our clients were good companies, very solid, nothing wrong with them. This market crash was a psychological avalanche, not a slide in the values of the companies.

Our phones were ringing nonstop, our clients were so terrified. To every client who called I said, "Just sit tight. Your companies are not going to go out of business tomorrow. If we don't sell, we won't lose."

Despite what my sense of reason knew to be true, that was still the most terrifying day I experienced in the financial industry. When I got home that night, I felt like I'd had a terrible case of diarrhea all day. In effect, that's what had happened to the market.

I was right, though. The companies we had invested in did not go out of business the next day. When the market had calmed down enough that our machines would give us stock quotes and we could get orders through, I could hear Yura Arkus-Duntov crowing in my ear, buy, buy, BUY! So we bought. Oh, we got some wonderful bargains in the second half of that October. Then a lot of other people figured out that most companies were just fine. They started buying again, prices rose again, and by the end of the year, the market was just above where it had started in January.

There are many theories about why the 1987 crash happened. One of the major theories was that people had been investing automatically through computer-generated programs and not really thinking through their investments, and I believe it. But if you really understand the market, you don't need theories. You only need to know how to run against the crowd. If everyone else is selling, buy, buy, BUY!

* * *

The crash of 1987 shocked me out of my depression. I could feel my next big adventure waiting for me. I started thinking, looking around, wondering... I was especially wondering if now might be a good time to expand. Finding brokers seemed like it would be a difficult thing to do; all of my brokers had found me. But it occurred to me that some companies did go out of business in the crash. Maybe some of them were brokerage firms?

I researched my idea and ding, ding! There it was: Fitzgerald DeArman Roberts (FDR) with offices in Irvine and La Jolla, California, Phoenix, Arizona, and Spokane, Washington. They had gone bankrupt and their brokers and clients were just sitting there doing nothing. I went to visit their offices and everything was in place, from the managers to the computer systems. They just didn't have the capital flow to get running again.

They were only too happy when I put in a bid. I was a smaller company than they had been, but if someone didn't buy them out they weren't going to be a company at all. I flew to Tulsa, Oklahoma, to negotiate with the NASD to take over the FDR offices. The NASD knew that if their brokers weren't placed properly and quickly, they'd be losing clients. They reviewed my financials in record time and basically rolled out a red carpet for me. Suddenly I had fifty brokers working for Yaeger Securities. The minnow swallowed the whale! I folded the FDR Irvine and La Jolla offices into my San Fernando office and kept the Phoenix and Spokane offices just as they were.

With this many brokers I realized that I needed a Chief Compliance Officer, so I hired David Mahler, a broker with a photographic memory who was studying for his law degree at night. His job at Yaeger Securities was to review all the brokers' trade tickets to make sure they complied with regulations.

He was invaluable in other ways, too. It was a major adjustment for my brokers to have a woman boss, even the ones who had come and asked to be hired by me. They knew I had the experience but they kept testing me to make sure I knew what I was doing. I had to prove myself to my own employees over and over. I ran out of time and patience for that. I asked David to work more with the brokers and run interference so I didn't have to deal with them directly as much. I now had more time to go out and find new business for my firm.

It was also a relief to bring a gentleman of outstanding

character on board, because I had recently discovered the truth about my Sales Manager. It turns out I had put a fox in charge of the chicken coop. Those limited partnerships he'd had years of experience with? He hadn't vetted them properly. He had also pushed them on clients who were not suitable for risky investments – people like retirees who needed to live on income from their investments. Some of my brokers had been playing by his playbook, too, and doing the same thing – disregarding suitability and not investigating the deals, mainly real estate transactions, thoroughly enough. The limited partnerships started to default. My sales manager's clients – our clients – were furious, understandably, and some of them began to sue him.

I was upset. Oh boy, was I upset. I fired him as fast as a gunshot, that fox. I'm not sure anyone had ever lied to me, to my face, for so long, about anything. I guess I was wrong to accept someone at face value.

My ex-sales manager was not the only fox in town. In 1988 the Securities and Exchange Commission sued Drexel Burnham Lambert. The Commission had been investigating the firm for several years, concentrating specifically on Michael Milken's high-yield bond trading department – Stephen's department.

Very few people had ever understood what Milken was doing. In the late 1980s the SEC, New York District Attorney Rudy Giuliani, and even Drexel itself had decided to investigate him, just in case his unorthodox but legal transactions were covering up any unorthodox and illegal transactions. Milken put up a wall of lawyers but the multiple investigations hammered away at him.

I had my own reason for hating Milken's department at that time. I had heard through the financial industry grapevine that they had fired Stephen.

The news was a huge shock. By all reports, Stephen had brought them a lot – and I mean a lot – of business. With his level of success, what on earth could he have done to deserve being fired? No one could tell me... But shortly before he was fired, Stephen had been diagnosed with AIDS.

Oh, it happened. It wasn't right and it wasn't legal, but it happened all the time back then. Stephen's homosexuality wasn't a surprise to me, but I guess it was to Drexel Burnham Lambert.

I was angry at Drexel and disgusted with Milken, especially when his 98-count indictment came down the following year. But much more than anything else, I was afraid for Stephen, and overwhelmed by grief. The really good, highly effective drug cocktails hadn't been invented yet. Back then, an AIDS diagnosis was a death sentence.

It was time for me to talk to Stephen. It was long, long past time, but he had never been willing so I had stopped trying. Now I started calling and leaving him messages. There was no reply. I sent him letters in the mail. There was no reply.

I kept trying.

Then more foxes appeared at Yaeger Securities. (I have to say, when you trust someone and it works out, that is a wonderful thing. I trusted David Mahler completely and he repaid me with honesty, integrity, and dedication to the good of the firm.) About six months after I took over Fitzgerald DeArman Roberts, I sent David up to

Spokane. The Spokane manager had been checking the brokers' trades for compliance, but I wanted David to do a double-check.

"Norma," he called me up, "you're not going to like this."

"Oh no. Don't tell me."

Shirley looked over. She could tell something was wrong.

"They're trading penny stocks up here. Buying stocks, selling them two days later. Most of them are losing money. There's going to be lawsuits if we don't do something about this."

I was so angry I could have growled. I had told them from the start that I took a true investor's approach to the market, looking for solid, long-term value. The short-term philosophy was not welcome in my brokerage firm. They either weren't using their brains or they had lost their minds, trading junk in my company.

"Give them a warning, David," I said.

He did. They did not change their way of doing business. So I closed the Spokane branch.

Then David discovered that the Phoenix brokers had been doing the same thing. One particular trader down there had been giving the guys "trading ideas," which basically amounted to speculative deals. All of his "ideas" were disasters. We warned them; they ignored it; we closed them down.

I may sound calm and collected about this now but it was a huge stress for me at the time. I always related to people personally – never reducing them to just numbers on a balance sheet – and I was all too aware that I was putting brokers out of work when we transferred their clients' accounts to the California office and closed their branches. For the good of the clients and the company it had to be done, but I worried and suffered the entire two years it took to complete the process. I don't like being the bad guy, even when I'm being the good guy and it's only the wrongdoers who think I'm the bad guy.

The brokers pushed back, complaining to their managers, begging for more time, but they had had their chance. I would not stand for unethical behavior with our clients' money.

CHAPTER NINE
There Is No Limit

I WASN'T DONE with new adventures. Buying FDR was just a little jaunt compared to the next journey I embarked on – and this venture was going to have a much longer, much happier life.

In January of 1989, bill AB-1933 became law for California. This bill was the brainchild of Maxine Waters, a state Assemblywoman at the time. (Two years later she would be elected to the U.S. House of Representatives where she still is today, over two decades later.) In 1987 California had put into effect Ms. Waters's legislation barring the state from investing state funds in the stocks or bonds of any company doing business with apartheid South Africa. With bill AB-1933 Ms. Waters was breaking new ground again; her priorities were outstanding.

AB-1933 ordered that of California's state government public contracts, fifteen percent had to be awarded to minority-owned businesses and five percent awarded to women-owned businesses. If any state department in charge of awarding contracts did not meet these requirements, they had to demonstrate that they had made a "good faith effort" to do so.

Ms. Waters's original version of the bill had set the percentages at 20 for women and 20 to 40 for minorities, but the fact that the bill was passed into law at all was impressive. An earlier federal executive order had simply been ignored by most of the United States, and there was quite a bit of opposition to bill AB-1933. At issue were three billion dollars in state contracts and four billion dollars in bonds annually granted by the state. (In today's dollars, that's over twelve billion.) About forty percent of the population of California was a racial minority, yet minorities and women combined were only receiving twelve percent of the contracts.[4]

Opponents squawked that there weren't enough qualified minority- and women-owned businesses available to satisfy those requirements. They also argued that the bill wasn't fair, that society should be color-blind and should treat men and women equally. Well, the situation as it stood wasn't fair and Ms. Waters's bill was trying to fix that. Yes, society should be treating everyone equally, but society obviously wasn't. The playing field was not even. Assumptions – some of them conscious, some of them unconscious – that people had about minorities and women affected a person's chances of even getting a foot in the door. I had been facing those biases for almost thirty years. Society needed to be taught how to behave equitably, and that's what legislation like this was for.

As to whether there were enough qualified companies available, that was an old argument that had been dis-proved many times. The problem wasn't with the available

---

4   Statistics from "Affirmative Action Bill Aids Minority Firms," Tina Bachemin, Black Enterprise, December 1988, p.22.

companies. It was with people's definitions of "qualified," tainted by their assumptions and biases.

The bill passed and the backlash began. But so did the business. I knew this was my biggest chance yet to grow my firm, and I leaped for it. I wanted to service California's pension plans.

Yaeger Securities was already working for investment managers of major mutual funds, as well as doing transactions for well-known international companies such as the Nomura Securities Company, Ltd., founded in Japan in 1925. This was a level of business that should impress any pension plan investment manager, as well as the fact that Merrill Lynch (Broadcort Capital) was clearing for us.

Instead of expanding Yaeger Securities, however, I decided to open a separate brokerage firm, Yaeger Capital Markets. The actions of the brokers at Yaeger Securities had resulted in lawsuits from their clients, bringing me headaches and sometimes tears. I wouldn't need brokers at all for Yaeger Capital Markets, just traders. I decided to make a clean break with my original firm and run two separate companies.

The application process was much easier this time around. After all, not only was the National Association of Securities Dealers already monitoring one company for me, I had nearly three decades of experience by now. The amount of risk was also much lower when working with institutions. Investment managers are paid to make the investment decisions, so they give brokerage firms unsolicited orders. We wouldn't have to pitch them on investing opportunities; we would just do the transactions for them. That diminished liability and made a firm more respectable in the eyes of the NASD.

The one thing I had to be absolutely certain to do was separate the two companies in the eyes of the public in every way – right down to having separate office doors with separate nameplates, and separate SIPC memberships for those nameplates. We also had to have a separate contract with Merrill Lynch to clear for us, but that was easy to negotiate. I'd be registered with both firms, and I would be the principal and the financial principal for Yaeger Capital Markets as well as, after taking another exam for a new license, the principal of municipal bonds. David Mahler registered with both firms, too, and became a financial principal.

There was only one hitch to the whole process, and this one was personal. For Yaeger Capital Markets to satisfy the requirement of being one hundred percent woman-owned, Larry would have to sign over his community property rights. Those rights guaranteed that if I died or divorced Larry, he would own half of the company. Some men would never sign that away, and for those who did, it could become a bone of contention. (I have one friend whose husband capped a divorce battle with a lawsuit over that exact issue.)

Larry and I had been married and in love for almost twenty years and he had always been enthusiastic about my career, but I was still a little nervous to ask him for this. Larry was very smart about money; I loved that about him. Doubling his money on Elba stock had brought us together, after all. But we both had a feeling that Yaeger Capital Markets was going to do very well. What if he didn't want to give up his rights?

"Of course I'll sign them over," Larry said with a huge smile. I guess he trusted me!

One of the other important things I needed was the right address for my office. When a busy manager at a very large institution gets a call out of the blue from a name he doesn't recognize, asking for his business, if he hears the wrong address he might think, "Eh, too small, ignore them." Plus, the biggest institutions would send someone to visit your office to make sure you were legitimate before they would sign any contracts. The other big brokerage firms were in downtown Los Angeles so I moved our trading desks there, to 550 South Hope Street. I signed a ten-year lease, too – hope indeed, and chutzpah, too. I also bought a new fax machine. The old one in the Encino office was just too big to move so we left it there.

The NASD approved the Yaeger Capital Markets application in 1991, ten years after I opened Yaeger Securities. My new firm was ready for clients – which I didn't have. And I didn't have referrals for any large institutions either. No matter how far you go in this industry, everything still comes down to cold calls.

I believe in going to the top, so I decided that my first potential client would be CalPERS – the California Public Employees' Retirement System. This pension plan was on its way to having one million members and up to one hundred billion dollars in its portfolio (benchmarks it would achieve a few years later). The prestige of transacting their orders from their portfolios would be enormous. It would make Yaeger Capital Markets a contender right out of the gate. I looked up their Senior Manager in a directory of investment managers and pension plans, and gave his office a call, absolutely cold.

If his office didn't give me an appointment, I would have called again. And again. I had a very thick skin after years of rejection. Rejection makes you stronger. It makes you a fighter. I would ask myself, why am I being rejected? What are the things I can do to change that? When it came to cold calling, I realized that people usually rejected calls because I was a total stranger. Well, without a referral, I could at least figure out ways to get them to recognize my name. I simply called enough times to make my name sound familiar and eventually I'd get an appointment.

Actually, to be honest, CalPERS might have been a different case. My firm was so small compared to the other brokerage firms competing for their business. I might have given up trying to get in touch with the CalPERS Senior Manager just because it seemed impossible.

However, his office did give me an appointment, right away. I am certain that I got that appointment because of bill AB-1933. I was perfectly qualified to do business with CalPERS, but the requirement that they consider woman-owned firms opened a door for me that would very likely have been tightly shut.

The location of the CalPERS Senior Manager's office was in Sacramento. Sometimes fog made it impossible for planes to land there, so I decided to fly up the night before the meeting and stay in a hotel to ensure being on time. I reviewed the package of materials that I would be presenting several times before I left my office and one more time at the hotel.

On the day of the meeting my eyes opened without an alarm clock at 4:00 in the morning, as usual, since my body was timed to be awake for the market opening. I immediately felt nervous, not because I wasn't prepared – I was thoroughly prepared – but because I didn't know what I was in for. What if this man had been opposed to the affirmative action legislation? What if his response to the state law was, "That's a bunch of bull, nobody's going to tell me what to do!"

Some of my confidence returned when I pinned my brooch on my suit in the hotel room. Hats were long out of style and California was too warm for them anyway, but I would always be the Hat and Brooch Lady at heart.

I remember the CalPERS office as being very new, very modern, a wide open feeling with lots of glass. I was still nervous as I waited in the lobby, but I knew what to do about that feeling – ignore it and get the job done. I went over in my mind what I needed to accomplish in the meeting. I never knew how much time I'd have to pitch, so I always made sure to deliver the most important facts in the first ten minutes. I knew the Senior Manager needed information about my certification, capability, and clearing. Yaeger Capital Markets was fully certified as a woman-owned company by the state of California. Merrill Lynch was clearing for us. And I had thirty years of experience with transactions and clients in England, Germany, and Japan as well as across the United States – if that wasn't capability, I didn't know what was. I had been working my whole life to get to this pitch.

The door of the Senior Manager's office opened and the secretary ushered me in. Here we go...

And he was warm and welcoming! In fact, he was very enthusiastic, pleasant, and charming. He listened to my pitch, then gave me a tour around the office and showed me their trading room. "To tell you the truth," he said, "I didn't know what I was going to do. I was scratching my head, trying to figure out where I could find qualified woman-owned brokerage firms. You're doing me a big favor, thank you for calling me!"

He couldn't order his investment managers to hire my firm for their securities transactions, but he was the kingpin of the plan and he agreed to give me a letter of introduction. I would still need to pitch to as many of the CalPERS investment managers as I could meet, but his letter was going to carry a lot of weight. Going home, I was flying higher than the jet.

I barely touched ground again for years. I made a staggering number of cold visits for Yaeger Capital Markets. I flew all over the country, starting with Sacramento again, this time to pitch to the California State Teachers' Retirement System (CalSTRS) – successfully! – and then to New York to pitch to some of the investment managers for both CalPERS and CalSTRS. For New York I would take a red-eye to LaGuardia Airport, land in the morning, meet an investment manager in a hotel across from the airport, and fly home to L.A., getting home around midnight. That twenty-four-hour whirlwind trip happened many, many times.

Even I was astonished at the energy I had, but to tell you the truth, I was having fun. It was incredibly satisfying to convince all these managers of large institutions to work with my little company, which didn't stay little for long. Having CalPERS and CalSTRS as my clients gave my firm a lot of credibility and opened up doors everywhere. Through them I connected with the California State Treasury office where Kathleen Brown, the sister of former governor (now the current governor again) Jerry Brown, got Yaeger Securities on board in the municipal bond business. Soon Yaeger Securities was in the Treasury office's prospectus and on the wall, too, where they display a list of their bond offerings.

Kathleen also made sure I attended the annual meeting of all the State Treasurers in the country. Each state takes a turn to see if it can out-do the previous year's party. There was a lobster fest in Maine, fly-fishing with an instructor on the Yellowstone River in Wyoming, and in Utah, a slalom ski race. I was just a beginner – well, Larry would say I was a poor skier, and he's right. I signed up for that ski race anyway.

The lift ride up that hill seemed very, very long. I had a perfectly clear view of what I was supposed to race down – every bump, every flag, and a slope that was much steeper than I wanted it to be. I had only just finished my skiing lessons. This race was certainly going to be my exam.

About ten people had gathered at the top of the slalom course, plus Larry, who was there to encourage me. And I needed encouragement about every ten seconds. "You'll be fine!" he said over and over. "Just go slowly."

I waited and agonized as I watched each contestant take their turn, gliding down the hill as the stopwatch rolled. Finally it was my turn. I was last and, judging by the skills I had just seen everyone demonstrate, definitely least. I shuffled over, not gracefully, to the starting line and looked down the hill.

Oh my god, am I crazy? I thought.

But it didn't matter if I wasn't good at skiing. I had to do this. I had to show I was a good sport to myself, and to everyone else, too.

"Get ready," said the announcer. "Get set..." And the bullhorn blew. I was off.

Really, really slowly, I was off.

I was fine until I hit the first bump. I really hadn't wanted to do that. It wobbled me, but I stayed upright. I also vowed to stay as far away as possible from every bump for the rest of the hill. So I started making my turns very, very wide. That slowed me down but not enough, so I turned in my toes and knees, putting my skis in "snowplow" position – the beginner's way of slowing down and stopping.

That didn't slow me down enough, either, though, especially when the slope got steeper, so I turned my knees in even more. Halfway down the slope my feet were probably pointing right at each other. Time was crawling by.

And that was good! I liked that! Slow was good. Every bump was a new challenge, but I took them one at a time, concentrating only on coming out of each bump still standing.

It seemed like a year later that I slid – well, more like oozed, considering the speed I was going – across the finish line. I was dead last in the race but I was standing up! That's all I had really cared about. Doing it was the important thing, not the winning or losing. You have to take a bite out of life, even if it scares you to death. Everyone applauded and cheered as I crossed the finish line, and that night at dinner, they made a big deal out of giving me the booby prize.

And the rest of the weekend, a lot of people gave me business for YCM, because after that race everyone at the meeting knew who I was. Ever since my conversation with my cousin Matty about my wardrobe, I have found ways to stand out and be noticed. That's important for any business that involves sales. You've got to make an impression and you have to have a hook to do that – even if it's the booby prize.

Over the years, Yaeger Securities continued to be a problem – many problems, in fact. Almost as many problems as I had brokers. I didn't understand what had happened to the mentality of stockbrokers over the years. They were promising clients the world but brokers are not supposed to offer guarantees. It's misleading and it encourages clients to fall for speculative "deals." When those deals fell through, the clients sued.

Yaeger Capital Markets, however, was successful and yes, fun, for as long as I was its principal. All those pitch meetings introduced me to truly wonderful people around the country. The State Treasurers were very helpful in giving me referrals and recommendations. (Mary Landrieu of Louisiana was especially helpful.) States across the country had copied Maxine Waters's legislation, so I cold called every pension plan I could find in the pension plan directory, teachers' plans, firemen's plans, police officers' plans, you name it. I was helping the institutions to be equitable in their business practices, and I'm very proud of that. After working with me, they were more open to working with other women executives and small firms.

Best of all, Yaeger Capital Markets brought me Loretta Sanchez. In the early days of YCM Loretta's husband was one of my traders. I found out that Loretta was packaging municipal bond offerings for the state of California. In fact, she was one of the earliest advisors to municipalities that were using Mello-Roos bonds, which allowed homeowners in a district to volunteer for a special tax on their property values. The revenue from that tax went toward municipal bonds that financed the building of schools, libraries, roads, and other institutions that would improve their neighborhood.

I arranged to meet Loretta and we got along very well, so I hired her as a consultant for Yaeger Securities. Loretta was one of the few people I have met who works as hard as I do. It was a real pleasure to work with her, and a few years later I was a little sad to learn that I was losing her – but happy to find out her reason. She was considering running for Congress. I told her emphatically, "Go to it!" I loved that she had such drive and vision, and I could imagine how great she would be as a Congresswoman. She was very bright, very astute. She'd be able to thoroughly analyze the bills that crossed her desk, and she could be trusted to make good decisions.

It didn't take her long to decide to do it. I hosted parties for her and helped her fundraise for her election. She was elected in 1996 and ever since, she has been re-elected for California's 47th Congressional District every two years. I missed her around the office but I was so proud of her. The country has been very lucky to have her service all these years.

Then and Now
Congresswoman Loretta Sanchez
speaks about Norma[5]

Before I met Norma, I was already impressed with her because of how she was helping my husband. He was working for her as a trader, which is the kind of job you can wear shorts for; it's all done on the phone. But Norma put him in a suit, pushed him to go to school and earn licenses that would make him more multi-dimensional, and brought him out on visits with potential clients to teach him how to pitch the business.

I was a dealmaker in the financial industry, Norma was a deal-seller, so one day we started talking and we decided we could work together and get more done. There were so few women in investment banking then, only two or three dealmakers at most. It was amazing to me that a woman owned her own investment brokerage firm.

There was little camaraderie among the women in the banking industry, too. The women were afraid to help each

---

5   In a telephone interview with Clare Kent, June 2011

other because it might diminish them in some way. Norma really helped women, though. She taught directly, she taught by example, and she gave opportunities to women. Norma was also fortunate to find women outside the industry who would help her, such as Mary Landrieu, former Treasurer for Louisiana, who became a U.S. Senator the same year I became a Representative. Mary was very instrumental in making sure there was a base of work for Norma.

But Norma understood that while women needed to help women, the financial industry was mainly comprised of men. We needed to search out the men who would help, too. Norma was never afraid to ask for help or receive it. It was equal-opportunity camaraderie.

Having already worked in the industry for five or so years, I knew that most men assumed from the beginning that a woman couldn't do the job. As a woman you had to be impressive from the first moment. When they gave you a chance they only gave it to you once, so you had to do twice as much homework and be extra prepared. It's still very, very true today: a woman has to work twice as hard as a man.

What I learned from Norma was how to be aggressive – not aggressive in a bad way, but fearless. She was wonderful to watch because she had a lot of guts. It was very difficult to go up against the men and the big firms, the big names like Goldman Sachs and Bear Stearns. Norma showed me how to be brave, which is half the battle. She'd say, "Let's go over there and get in the mix!"

She was always thoroughly prepared in a very strategic way. She would think about what she was going after and all the different ways she could get to that. She focused. She asked herself, "Who do I know, how can I angle to get to the person or thing that I want?" Then she would make multiple attempts at the same problem or opportunity. Even when she would fail, she already had two or three other ways to get what she wanted. She was never discouraged.

Norma taught me that if you fail at one attempt, you can't go away, you have to try again. That has been incredibly important for me as a U.S. Representative. Business in Congress is personality-driven and it's frustrating. There's a very long process to pass a piece of legislation. The almost automatic answer from anyone is, No, I can't do that. So I strategize like Norma: how can I push at different pressure points to get it done?

Norma knew that she was breaking the glass ceiling in a lot of ways and going to places that women had never reached before. But at the time, I don't think she realized the impact she was making on the people around her. She just had the determined guts to go out and get the job done. We were in a business that required us to have gumption without arrogance, and she had that. I'm very fortunate to have worked with her.

CHAPTER TEN
The Roller Coaster

1993 DID NOT BEGIN auspiciously. Rudolf Nureyev died soon after the new year began. Margot Fonteyn had passed away two years earlier. The dynamic duo who had been so inspiring to me was just history now – but what a history.

My own dynamic career, however, was on another upswing. The Stratosphere Corporation was going to build the tallest observation tower in the world, and I was in on the ground floor.

It was 1993 and Stratosphere had hired Yaeger Securities to be its sole sales agent. Our job was to sell stock in the corporation to raise over thirty-two million dollars for its future casino/hotel in Las Vegas.

It was such a thrill to see the drawings of the tower that would be attached to the casino. The graceful, swooping sides of the tower seemed so slender as they rose to the jeweled cap on top. It looked like a statuette presented at some fabulous awards ceremony.

And for me, in a way, it was an award. It was not common for a corporation to hire only one sales agent; this was a privilege. It restored my confidence in Yaeger Securities at a time when those terrible limited partnership deals were bringing in lawsuits. I would also be eligible for an underwriter's warrant, which meant that after a certain amount of time, I would have the opportunity to buy Stratosphere stock for a fraction of the share price.

Although I would be selling the Stratosphere stock as an intangible since the casino was still under construction, somehow this felt like the most tangible offering I had ever worked with. The drawings made it seem real, as well as the visits to Las Vegas to see the earth being moved around the giant construction site. I looked up at that enormous desert night sky and imagined the tower's crown sparkling against it.

The tower also represented a kind of funny handshake between my New York past and my California present: California because it was a real estate venture, and New York because at the time, the construction plans included an external elevator to carry sightseers up the side of the tower – an elevator made to look like a giant ape, just like King Kong climbing the Empire State Building. The New York New York casino wasn't built yet so that ascending ape was as Manhattan as you were going to get in Vegas (except, of course, for the Frank Sinatra days).

The job was so big I had to hire more brokers to help with the selling. That wasn't difficult to do since stocks for a casino in Las Vegas was one of the more fun issues a broker could represent, and not too much of a challenge to sell. Casinos seemed to be one of the few industries that were unaffected by the recession of the early '90s, at least for investors. Plenty of people wanted in on the new glory of the Strip. The Mirage had opened in 1989, attracting a new crop of investors to Vegas. The great green MGM Grand had finished its external construction in early 1993, and Luxor was being built at the same time as Stratosphere.

I established my new stable of brokers and at the end of June the Stratosphere Corporation delivered their prospectus to us. That document was the official starting gunshot for our selling race. We were off and running!

One morning two months later, a fire broke out at the Stratosphere construction site. The whole tower, halfway built and already dominating the skyline, went up in flames. No one was hurt and the concrete that had been poured for the tower wasn't damaged, but that lovely award was now a liability. The construction project and, by extension, the corporation were thrown into upheaval. They weren't back to square one, thanks to that concrete, but this was a huge setback. On our end, no stock could be sold in the Stratosphere Corporation until they had updated their prospectus to include a description of the fire, as required by law.

It took them a month to update the prospectus. Doesn't sound like a long time, does it? Except that I had to keep paying salaries to all those extra brokers I had hired. That tore right through the capital I had on hand for Yaeger Securities, nearly bankrupting my firm. In fact, it sent me humbly to the telephone to ask my brother Harvey if he would lend me fifty thousand dollars. Fortunately, he agreed. I put the money into the Yaeger Securities capital and met my obligations to my brokers.

I also made sure to pay Harvey back, with interest. In my life I have borrowed quite a bit of money, and being able to do that gave me the ability to start over again, several times. I don't think a person can succeed at anything without borrowing money at some point, and our country won't grow if people can't borrow. That's why the financial industry is so important. The industry makes it possible for banks to make loans. Banks that simply sit on their funds without lending them out – as many of them are doing now in 2012 – are holding the country back.

As soon as the Stratosphere prospectus had been updated, we could start selling again. It's not so easy, though, selling shares for a casino that's just had a fire and has delayed its opening date. In addition, the Grand Casinos corporation bought an enormous percentage of the shares – very good for Stratosphere but far fewer shares for us to sell. It took us a year and a half, but we persisted and sold all the shares.

However, by the time our underwriters' warrants would have kicked in, the Stratosphere Corporation had declared bankruptcy. Carl Icahn took control of the company and, of course, eventually Stratosphere became very successful indeed. I estimate that my missed opportunity with them cost me two million dollars.

It turned out that when the Stratosphere tower opened, there was a roller coaster at the top of it. That was eventually dismantled but in 2010 they installed the SkyJump, which allows you to jump off the tower and fall for 829 feet. Between those two rides, that was pretty much how my experience with Stratosphere felt.

And they never did build that great ape elevator.

* * *

Back in 1993, Yaeger Securities didn't have a lock on bad news. Wilshire Savings and Loan was delivering, too.

In the 1980s the federal government had passed legislation that deregulated some of the actions of the Savings and Loans Associations (S&Ls). Given free rein, many of the S&Ls started to make wild investments that they didn't have enough expertise to manage, or enough capital to reduce the resulting risk – investments that were a far cry from the US Treasury Bills I had opted for when I was a director for Wilshire S&L.

My directorship with Wilshire was long over by 1993, but I was still an investor. Many of the S&Ls had gone bankrupt or been closed by the regulating agency, the Federal Deposit Insurance Corporation (FDIC, which had absorbed the former FSLIC). Wilshire was still standing, but barely. We had endless meetings about Wilshire's urgent need to raise more capital, but there was no way to do that. Nobody wanted to give the infusion of cash that it needed. Even the president of the S&L wasn't willing to do it and he was a wealthy man. I had $100,000 invested in Wilshire and I was very, very nervous about it.

* * *

As I faced up to all of these business problems, however, I knew that there was something much bigger, much more important, that I needed to take care of. Stephen had never answered any of my phone messages or letters. Finally, I decided to go to him in person.

I think I must have decided to go right from work that day because David Mahler drove me. We parked in front of Stephen's house and David didn't need to ask me, he already knew that I needed to do this alone. I walked up to the front door from the sidewalk, not knowing what to expect. I was so scared – of Stephen, a little bit, but mostly for Stephen. I rang the doorbell. I rang it several times.

A curtain was pulled aside from a window and there was Stephen, looking so thin, so sick. I had a horrible flashback to Nicole fighting cancer.

Stephen spoke through the closed window, "Go away. I don't want to see you." Then he let the curtain drop.

It was a knife in my heart.

I went back to the car alone. I sat in the passenger seat. I said nothing. David started the car and drove away while I cried.

It took me some time before I could try again. I was devastated. I was paralyzed with guilt. I could not imagine how I could change Stephen's mind.

But I did try again, in 1994. This time when I rang the bell, somebody I didn't know opened the door.

I said, "I'm not leaving until I see Stephen."

"He already passed away."

"What are you talking about?"

"They just took him to be cremated."

My son... my little boy who had built bed sheet fortresses with me when we were living by Lake Louise Marie that cold, lonely winter in 1961... the charming young man who seemed to have inherited all my skills in sales and added his own talent, too....

This is the deepest regret of my life. I have said to other people and I say again now, if you are in a situation where you are estranged from someone you love, go fix it. Now. Don't wait till it's too late.

I should have tried sooner, harder. I should have forced him to see me early on so that we could talk, even if the conversation would start with the old argument. We would have fought past the bad feelings and found common ground again. We would have made peace, before it was too late. But I missed him.

Twenty years later, time hasn't changed my terrible grief for him. It never will.

* * *

Filled with sadness and remorse, I fell into the arms of the rest of my family. Larry, of course – the love of my life, and the love *in* my life when I was bereft.

Our three eldest children had all met their mates in college and married happily. Victor and Susan were living in Arizona with their wonderful six-year-old, David. Susan had earned her MA in anthropology and museum studies and her PhD in educational psychology. She was very skilled and, while Victor was earning his MA and PhD in clinical psychology at Michigan State University, she was hired by the State of Michigan to work on the exhibit for their capitol rotunda. I had a lot of respect for her talent.

When they moved to Arizona, Victor opened his private practice in psychology and he was very well suited to the profession. He was warm and friendly with his patients and he listened well. He never took anything at face value; when he researched a problem he was thorough and tenacious and never rushed the answer. His ability to think long-term was just as important for therapy as for investing.

Most of all, Victor had the ability to make people feel special. That's how Doc Grossman had helped me; he taught me that my life was as important as anyone else's and that I had the right and the responsibility to live it. I told Victor a bit about Doc Grossman after he opened his practice and he felt the Doc had done a great job. It meant a lot to know that Victor was helping people in a way that I knew, first-hand, was so necessary.

Sheri and her husband, Bruce, had two daughters – Stacy, about the same age as David, and Callie, three years younger. Bruce was very smart and in demand in the computer industry; working for companies such as IBM and

Intel kept their family moving around for many years. Some wives would find that a real challenge to deal with, but not Sheri. Her chutzpah and decisiveness had never left her. That hadn't always made life easy for Larry and me when she was a teenager – she did what she thought was right! Larry and I made a pact that we would always back each other up with our children, even if we didn't agree with each other. Though Sheri would test us, she was very bright and she would listen to good sense when we delivered it. And of course I remembered testing my father the same way, maybe even more so, and being a better person for it.

Sheri's strong character was still serving her well. Every time Bruce was moved, Sheri found a new job in the new place, no problem. She was working on *pro forma* financial statements for hospitals and she was always bettering herself. If she wasn't satisfied with her advancement within an organization, she'd look for another opportunity and take it. Eventually she worked all the way up to being Chief Financial Officer of a nonprofit organization in San Diego.

Elysa met David in one of her classes at Cal State Northridge. They wanted to move in together but Larry and I objected to that – it wasn't a common practice then. So instead they got married, and that was a good choice; they were well suited for each other. They wanted children very much but they weren't sure whether they could have them. David was very successful at Pacific Bell, selling commercial telephone systems. (Later, when PacBell went through a merger and downsizing, David became a math teacher.) He also loved flying and had earned his pilot's license. Elysa worked in marketing for a while for some fine firms, including Speedo. Then at last, she conceived her miracles: lovely Naomi, born in 1990, and her brother Seth in 1993.

Elysa was a great mother, so warm-hearted and giving. She was so kind she would take in strays – stray puppies and people, too, friends or acquaintances who needed a little help or a couch to stay on. Elysa was also a really wonderful cook. She learned some of her skills from my mother but then taught herself more, bringing herself up to a whole new level. She would cook all the family's holiday meals and do any catering needed by the organizations she and David volunteered with. When I needed advice I called her, and it was always a treat to sit at her table.

Tod was a charmer, very personable with a great sense of humor. Once when he was at college I called him up to say that Larry and I were going to come visit with him.

"Oh," he said.

"What's the problem?" I said.

"Well, I'll have to clean my room but that's not the problem. The problem is, after you leave I'll have to mess it up again so I can live in it."

(Tod completely denies that this ever happened, but Larry and I remember it and love it.)

Tod put together a band with a few friends in California and recorded a few LPs, with him playing guitar. Then he moved to New York City and lived with his mother for a while before he set up an apartment of his own. That helped to heal the long-standing rift between the two of them, a very good thing. (Years later when she needed help, he was there to provide it.) Tod created his career by working his way up in a specialized foods company, eventually forming his own niche as a sales agent for high-end catering for law firms, brokerages, and other select commercial firms. He had a book of clients just like I did and he was doing very well.

Seeing my children happy and being able to hold my grandchildren – I was so thankful for that. I had tried to be strong for my family my whole life. Now they were lending their strength to me.

* * *

I needed that strength when the FDIC finally came knocking on Wilshire's door. Wilshire was one of the last S&Ls to go, but in 1995 the FDIC finally decided that it did not have enough capital to keep operating. They sued every principal director, present and past, including me. They told me that the investments I had made for the S&L were "incorrect investments."

"Are you kidding me?" I said. "US Treasury Bills? You can't find a safer investment than that! And you're calling my decision incorrect?" I was furious.

On top of that the FDIC, against my advice, immediately sold the Treasury Bills I had purchased with Wilshire's capital – selling them at the bottom of the market, which created a loss of $127,000. They wanted me, me personally, to reimburse them for that loss. If they had simply waited to sell, even for a few weeks, they would have generated a generous profit.

No way was I going to take this without a fight. David Mahler acted as my in-house lawyer, working with an outside attorney, and we went to work on the FDIC. In 1996 they dropped their demand down to $40,000. That still wasn't fair, considering that I had done nothing wrong, so I counter-offered. It took them another year to make a decision about that. In 1997, two years after they started the shutdown, my legal fees for the outside attorney were killing me. I owed my attorneys more than I owed the FDIC. I had to stop the bleeding. I had to settle.

I settled for $16,000, which I paid over two years (adding to my investment loss of $100,000 and all the funds that went to lawyers' fees). But most importantly, the FDIC agreed that my settlement would state in writing that I was not guilty of any wrongdoing.

Well, if I wasn't guilty, why did there have to be a settlement at all? Because the FDIC had to save face. They couldn't have spent all that money on their investigation and legal fees without having something to show for it.

* * *

Those were dark years, the early '90s. But what do you do? You keep moving. You scoop yourself up and move on to the next thing.

There was no shortage of "next things," thanks to Yaeger Capital Markets. I was unstoppable when it came to that firm. It had done nothing but soar since its very first flight. While David monitored the firm at home I continued to journey all over the country, finding new clients. We worked with the Teachers' Retirement Systems of California, Texas, and Louisiana, the Washington-Idaho Laborers-Employers Pension Trust, New York's TIAA-CREF, and the big men at the Chicago Firemen's Annuity and Benefit Fund. We worked with some of the biggest money management companies in the industry: Alliance Capital Management Corporation, Goldman Sachs Asset Management – Tampa, and J. & W. Seligman & Co. Inc., among many others. Once management companies realized YCM was a good firm to do business with, they recommended us to some of their other clients, which sent us even more work. And through our international money management firms, I began conducting transactions for managers servicing accounts in Malaysia, Singapore, and

Hong Kong, as well as England and Japan (with Broadcort Capital handling all the currency exchanges).

Larry and I decided that he should become a registered financial principal for Yaeger Capital Markets. If anything happened to me, we wanted to make sure that there would be no disruption in the business! He took all the classes he needed to pass the exam while still running his medical practice. And once he had the license and all the paperwork was finished, he came up with a new nickname for me: "Boss." I really was lucky to find him.

I can't imagine what life would have been like if YCM hadn't been such a success during this time. Knowing that I was excelling in that arena gave me resilience I might not otherwise have had.

It also gave me buoyancy when the axe fell on Yaeger Securities. I had certainly made the right decision to run them as separate firms.

Ten lawsuits against Yaeger Securities by 1997 totaled over half a million dollars, all thanks to that one Sales Manager who was such an accomplished liar that I didn't see through him until it was too late. The NASD required the firm to have $100,000 capital at all times, but I had to apply those funds to legal fees. The firm filed for bankruptcy in May of 1997.

And because I was a "control person" of the firm, I was jointly and severally liable, which meant that every lawsuit was a suit against me personally, as well as against the brokers and the firm. When we reached a settlement for $300,000, I had to file for personal bankruptcy – a Chapter 13. My personal share of the liability payments was $32,700, which I paid off in full over the next few years.

Bankruptcy – it's a terrible word. I was ashamed of it. I had to notify all the regulatory agencies of my firm's failure, and it appeared on all my financial statements and my license, as clear as day. I would sit and think as I filled out the paperwork, oh my god, how am I going to get through this?

But as I talked to people about it, I realized that bankruptcies are actually very common in the financial industry. They are not shameful; they are simply mistakes, that then you must learn from. One of the greatest things about America is that our country allows us to recover from failure. It takes more than one try to get all kinds of ventures right. Without the ability to declare bankruptcy, how could we pick ourselves up and start over – wiser and more prepared the second time around?

One gentleman I spoke to said, "If you didn't go bankrupt, you wouldn't know what it feels like to go bankrupt. It's important to experience these things in business, so that you understand that a bankruptcy is not the black mark you thought it was."

Folding Yaeger Securities didn't dent my reputation at all, and I do think it was important for those clients to get some kind of recompense for the actions of my Sales Manager. I just needed to learn how to get over the hump of my fear and embarrassment, like any other humbling experience in life, and demonstrate that I had learned from my mistakes.

Eventually I just felt great relief. Finally, finally, that firm with so many headaches and heartaches and problems, was off my back. It took me about a year to pay off my Chapter 13 debts, and then I was free to concentrate fully on Yaeger Capital Markets. That's where my heart and mind were.

Then and Now
David Mahler, Esq., speaks about Norma[6]

When I went to work for Norma, brokerage firms wanted their employees to work all hours, and that's still true today. Norma, however, enthusiastically supported my plan to study law at night and arranged my schedule so I could.

There were hardly any brokerage firms headquartered in Los Angeles in the early '90s, and a woman executive was even less common. The financial industry was still a good old boys' club. The trading rooms in most brokerage firms were piranha tanks. In fact, most companies didn't allow women in their trading rooms because they knew the culture, they knew what went on there (for example, bringing in exotic dancers during business hours). If a woman did work in a trading room, she usually only lasted a couple of weeks.

Norma's trading room was very different. The traders at Yaeger Capital Markets were professional and dedicated.

The brokers at Yaeger Securities were a different story. Brokers are sort of a different breed in general, but even among brokers, these people were quirky, even strange. That didn't affect their work, though, until they started going crazy with the limited partnership deals. Those deals made huge money and a lot of the brokers weren't even thinking about the suitability of the deals for their clients. Later, after the deals collapsed and the lawsuits started coming in, some of the brokers pleaded ignorance; but how can you *not* think about whether your client needs his or her retirement income to live on? The brokers were just greedy.

---

6   In a telephone interview with Clare Kent, March 2012

Norma wasn't like that at all, which is why she enjoyed Yaeger Capital Markets so much more – no brokers, no clowns. She didn't have to worry about being lied to or getting sued. Yaeger Capital Markets was a real brokerage firm and Norma was very reasonable to work with. She was assertive and she had a strong will but if you told her something was in her best interest, she would listen to you and take your advice. In the securities industry, those traits made her a very good manager. She was also an outstanding salesperson – very motivated and very persistent.

I'm grateful that she trusted me and made it possible for me to learn one industry while preparing for another. I'm still doing legal work for the financial industry and Norma and I are still friends today.

CHAPTER ELEVEN
Bareboating

LARRY AND I were having dinner at our home one evening when Larry said, "Boss, I'd like you to consider something."

"This sounds familiar," I joked. "Are you going to say something about getting married? Again?"

He laughed and said, "If you want me to!" Then he added, more seriously, "No, this might be bigger than that."

It was 1997. The worst of the Yaeger Securities bankruptcy procedure was over and I was happily piloting Yaeger Capital Markets through its continued success. I was pretty sure there wasn't anything Larry would say to me that could be a problem.

"What's on your mind?" I said.

"I was right about moving to California, wasn't I?"

"One hundred percent," I said.

"Well, you're the boss, but I've been making this list in my head of all the places we've never been, Australia, South America, most of Europe. You've been to Asia on business —"

"And we've seen a lot of the U.S. ..."

"Very true," he said. I had tried to bring Larry to as many of the State Treasurers' annual meetings as I could, for example. "But Norma, there is so much else in the world we should see, don't you think?"

"I guess so. Yes, you're right."

"But as long as you have to be in the office, we can't take enough time to go see them."

He was right there, too. Larry had retired two years before but the most I could be away from the office was a week, and I really wasn't comfortable taking more than a long weekend.

"And," he continued, "you're sixty-seven." We smiled at each other. The number just didn't seem right. I felt so much younger. "Norma," he said, "I'm asking you to consider retiring. I know that your career has made you so happy over all these years, but please give it some thought."

Well, I was surprised at my reaction. I didn't break into tears or rage. I couldn't say I was overjoyed at the idea, but after all, he wasn't asking me to be a homemaker. He was asking me to do something I'd always wanted to do more of: travel. See the world with my husband and partner at my side – not a bad way to live at all. Once again I could feel that great force of Change.

"OK, I'll think about it, Larry."

He looked relieved. He must have been expecting worse...

I did think about it and I realized he was completely right. Thirty-five years in business was long enough. I had places to go, sights to see – I wanted to go around the world! I told Larry yes.

"But," I said, "on one condition. YCM is doing so well, I don't want to close it down. I want to sell it if I can."

He agreed that that was sensible. I started looking for a buyer and he started going over the list of destinations in his head, trying to figure out where to go first.

Selling YCM took me a little longer than either of us expected. To keep all the pension plans and other affirmative action clients, the firm had to be either 100% woman-owned or 100% minority-owned. In addition, as usual, my standards were sky-high. YCM was the greatest achievement of my career and I wasn't going to trust it to just anyone. I searched for a solid year.

One day I mentioned it over lunch to a woman who was a money manager and she gave me a response I'd heard several times: "You *really* would retire?" Nobody ever believed me.

"Yes," I said. "I've achieved. It's enough. I'm happy with my life."

I felt such gratitude for being able to say that statement and mean it. Not everyone gets the help they need – the Doc Grossmans, the Earls, the Larrys – to make their lives turn out so well.

The money manager grilled me a little more but I convinced her I meant it. Then she called up an acquaintance of hers, Michelle Morton Schoeffel, a licensed investment advisor who was working for Mellon Bank in their investment management department. Michelle phoned me and said that she and her husband, who worked in the brokerage business, had a client who might be willing to put up the funds to purchase Yaeger Capital Markets. Was I really interested?

I really was, especially when I met her. Michelle, an African-American woman in her mid-thirties, made a great impression from the first moment. She was very bright, lively, dressed well, and she was very qualified. She knew the market. She was on top of what was happening with it and she could speak to people about it – the two most important skills for acquiring and retaining clients. I was extremely impressed. And she had a big company willing to be her backer for the deal. In short, she was exactly what I'd been looking for.

So in 1998, I sold Yaeger Capital Markets to the company Michelle and her husband founded, Pacific American Securities. To this day, the firm is going strong under Michelle's leadership.

The deal was originally going to be a five-year buyout, but then Michelle offered to pay me the lump sum in advance if I would take a discount. I thought about it and the market was volatile at that time so I said, "You know what? Cash is king. I don't know what's going to happen to me tomorrow. I'll take the advance payment!" It was a nice offer and I felt good taking it.

Michelle also asked me to stay for one more year after the company officially changed hands, to counsel and advise her and to represent the firm at national conferences, as I had always done. That, too, made me feel great. (I've kept my licenses to this day so that I can continue to be her ambassador as needed.)

Michelle's purchase had included taking over my office leases, so it was very odd to walk into my own office on the day the nameplate on the door was changed to Pacific American Securities. And I admit, there were times I sat in my office and wondered how I could let go of my company, my baby. So much of my identity had been this industry and specifically this firm. I had to tell myself when a decision was made by Michelle instead of by me, "This isn't mine."

Being able to watch Michelle at work for a year, though, put any worries I had to rest. She was every bit as wonderful as I'd thought she'd be, an excellent person to pass the torch to.

In a way, I had been sharing my torch for years, hoping that other women would run with it. Way back in the early years of Yaeger Securities, I had started to give a specific lecture at all the conferences. I titled it "A Woman's Approach" and my goal was to involve more women in the market. In the early 1980s there weren't too many people in the audience, just a few wives who had accompanied their husbands because the conferences were usually at vacation-type locations like Chicago, New Orleans, Key West. I remember one woman raising her hand and asking me, "My husband takes care of all this, what can I do?"

"Shouldn't you know what he's doing, though?" I said. "In the event you have to take over some day?"

Another woman said, "We just have our accountant do it all."

"Then check up on him!" I said. "Watch what he's doing and make sure he's doing the right thing for you. Does he have your future objectives in mind?"

I let them sit with that for a minute. Then I said, "Let me ask you this: why did you attend this lecture instead of going shopping? That's what most of the attendees' wives do."

They laughed a little bit and then one woman said, "I'm bored with shopping. I need to learn more about investing."

I said, "Good! Let's talk about picking stocks."

I taught them what to look for, what to do, what not to do, and how to do it. I encouraged them to come speak to brokers before they made investment decisions, to pick a broker's brain and understand all the reasoning behind choosing a particular stock. Most importantly, I taught them not to hire a broker who was also being paid a commission from a third party. (The practice was just getting started then but it is very common today.) Usually the third party pays a commission to the broker for selling a particular investment product. If you pay the broker, too, that means the broker is getting paid twice. That's not fair and it's a conflict of interest. You should be paying for good advice, not advice that guarantees the broker's pocket will be double-lined.

I also taught the attendees of my lectures not to work with the investment advisors of a bank because they are paid by the bank, which means they aren't really in the business. Asking them for advice is like going to a doctor who's just come out of medical school and hasn't done his internship or residency yet. Work with professionals who earn their livings by giving advice about the market, and your success will be their success.

As the 1980s rolled by, my audiences got bigger and the women in them got younger. They had college degrees, careers, and retirement savings, and they were excited to learn about the market and managing their money. I especially loved teaching them about investment clubs.

It can be tough to be an individual investor, if you're not working with a pot full of money. Doing small trades can incur penalties and the commissions can eat you alive. You're also less likely to be able to buy new issues of stock. An investor is much better off buying in bulk, so I encouraged women to pool their funds with their friends in investment clubs. They would all share the responsibility of the homework – doing the research of which stocks to buy – and would meet regularly to discuss what they learned. The head of the club could talk to a broker as needed for more information, then authorize the trades. Investment clubs grew in popularity and some of them even saw some fame for their successful rates of return (especially the Beardstown Ladies).

I find that on the whole, women are more conservative investors than men. Women aren't risk-takers as much. They're also more interested in learning and listening to what advisers have to say. They don't try to out-do a broker in a conversation. The market could use more of this conservative approach. It could balance out all the short-term traders and investors who think they can just surf the market.

And of course, the products today are different from back then. Exchange-traded funds, options, puts and calls, etc. – we didn't have all that. We just had stocks and bonds. Today's products seem designed to create a more risk-taking mentality and I don't think the market is better off for that.

Around the same time that I was teaching my seminars "A Woman's Approach" and "How to Select an Investment Manager," I met Bill Griffeth at one of the conferences. He had recently founded the Financial News Network on cable TV so I was delighted that he took my card. And I was thrilled that his production team called soon after: they wanted me to appear on his show. He had a Q&A period with call-ins from viewers and I would be the first woman to be featured on it.

I found TV to be easy. Maybe it was because I was so comfortable with my subject matter and so used to being at a podium after all those conferences. It was a pleasure to be fielding those phone calls, especially because I knew that women can find it hard to ask a man for investment advice. More than one had told me over the years, "Men make me feel stupid for asking questions." Many of those call-ins turned into clients, since the phone number for Yaeger Securities was on the screen under my name.

The office always saw a surge in business after one of my appearances on the show.

Bill Griffeth eventually moved to CNBC and has been a fixture there for years. Currently he is co-anchoring a show called *Closing Bell*. His co-anchor is a woman, Maria Bartiromo. She is frequently shown reporting from the floor of the New York Stock Exchange, where once upon a time, women weren't even allowed to enter.

It's important to understand just how shocking it would have been in the 1960s for people to see a woman reporting financial news on TV, never mind actually being at the stock exchange. When I was starting out in the business, a woman would have been serving Bill Griffeth his coffee and that's it. Now many of his commentators and guests are women, including CEOs. Griffeth really deserves credit for being open-minded enough to bring me onto his program twenty years ago, and for welcoming women into the world of finance reporting in all the years since.

In case it seems unnecessary or insignificant to honor those who made cultural changes like this over the last few decades, remember that there are still many people out there fighting against equal pay and other basic rights for women. The cultural change is not complete yet in this country, and unfortunately, taking steps backward is all too possible. "Those who don't know history are destined to repeat it."[7]

One evening after I appeared on Bill Griffeth's show, I came back to the office to hear a different kind of follow-up call on the answering machine: "Norma! I finally found you! I've been looking for you for years! I heard you on the TV and your voice was so familiar to me, I just had to look and see if it was you. And it was!"

---

7   Edmund Burke

BREAKING DOWN THE WALLS

The message was from an old childhood girlfriend of mine. Somehow we had lost track of each other after my divorce from Sam. She had married and moved to Florida but now here we were, reconnected after decades, thanks to Bill Griffeth and television. It didn't just reconnect me with a dear friend; it also made me realize that I really was reaching out into all corners of America with my message.

Michelle had received that message – Women, invest! Get involved! – maybe not from me specifically but somewhere along the line, the same message. She brought so much skill and good sense to Pacific American Securities, I could rest easy, handing over my firm to her. The office threw me a party on my last day there, and I felt such pride and optimism for the firm's future.

The next morning I woke up at – you guessed it – four a.m. I sat at my computer and did some research on the market – still do, today – and that morning I almost walked out of the house to get in the car for my commute down-town. Then I remembered, no more commute!

But so much distance to cover...

Larry had prioritized his list of destinations and chosen the first trip: a voyage literally around the world! First we flew from Los Angeles to China, back when China was all bicycles. (Now they have so many cars they've stopped issuing licenses. I've been back there since and I can't believe it's the same place.) We toured all around China, then took a cruise ship from Hong Kong to southeast Asia. Larry had always wanted to go to Mandalay to see "the flying-fishes play," as Rudyard Kipling described in his poem "Mandalay," so we visited Myanmar even though it was still under military rule at the time. Sadly, Larry didn't get to see any flying fish since the country is too far inland to have any. We were pleased just to see the country and how the people lived, though. How totally different their culture was from our world...

We also visited Singapore, Thailand, and Malaysia. Then we docked at Mumbai to take a land tour up through northern India for a flight out of New Delhi. Again, how different India was, how vibrant in color and crowds, unpredictable every day... and we could enjoy it all without getting sick, because we were very careful about our food and water. When we finally boarded our British Airways jet Larry said, "Thank goodness, now I can have a scotch on the rocks!" I had a drink with him to celebrate our grand global journey. Little did we know that the rocks were made with water from India. We spent three days in London on antibiotics before we could make it home to L.A.

But it was still a glorious trip, one of our most exciting and very much a dream come true.

There was so much more coming, though! A long, delicious tour through sun-dappled France. Iguazu Falls in Brazil – a massive, two-mile gorge filled with thundering waterfalls as high as skyscrapers. Eva Peron's tomb in Argentina. Safaris in Africa. A ground tour in Australia, where Sydney reminded us so much of California, Larry came out of a restaurant one evening and said, "Where did I park my car?" Ayers Rock glowing hot red in the desert sun. Waiting in New Zealand for herds of sheep to cross the roads before we could keep driving – that sure wasn't California.

Of course, in our travels we didn't neglect the glories that America has to offer. Larry signed us up for a river rafting tour of the American River in northern California. I wasn't the strongest swimmer but I was game for anything Larry suggested – he is a licensed lifeguard. The tour was also a tutorial for all the beginners like me, but nobody told me not to put sunscreen on the backs of my legs. The first bump in the water that our raft hit, me and my slippery self flew right out of the boat into the river. Good thing I was wearing my life jacket.

Very soon after that, the tour stopped near a hill to teach us how to get in and out of the water and save yourself. The guides wanted us to get used to being in the water so they had us all jump in from the top of the hill. Well, I jumped and then I just enjoyed being in the river, splashing and playing around. I saw Larry wildly waving at me but I had no idea why he was calling. Then he jumped in and started swimming hard – desperately, in fact. Without knowing it I'd been caught in a riptide, and Larry got to me just before I was going to go over a waterfall. If it hadn't been the American River, the easiest river in the West, I wouldn't have survived. Larry saved my life!

That's right, behind this great woman there was a great man, and I'm sure that's as universally true as the famous reverse of that statement. (Equal treatment, equal respect, and equal credit!)

Before I married Larry, I was scared to even look at the water. And after nearly dying many people would have stayed away from deep water; but not me. I never let a little failure in my career keep me down, why would I let this one stop me? That would have cramped my world. So Larry and I went on to raft almost every river in western America.

We also snorkeled and scuba dived all over the world. Oh, there was so much space and freedom around us when we did a dive... I imagine that must be what skydiving feels like. We also skied a great deal, but when Larry's hip went, he needed a hip replacement. He couldn't ski anymore so we took up sailing. Larry was so thorough in his training that he learned how to navigate so that he could captain a boat without needing a crew. That meant we could sail a ship bareboat by ourselves all around the Caribbean, and then in the South Pacific near Tonga and Tahiti.

That didn't mean we were done with cruises, though. We took a cruise ship from Tierra del Fuego all the way down to Antarctica! Oh that was indescribable. White so white it burned your eyes, white snow, white sky, white ice in the towering sides of the gorges looming over our little Zodiac motorboats. We saw an iceberg the size of Rhode Island down there – splendid! That was a very special trip. I'd come a long way from the Catskills, where I had hid in my borrowed house from snow and bears.

We have now been to every continent and on every ocean on the planet. Our travels are so exciting and so educational – what a reward for working so hard all those decades. I think of all those men and women around the world who have had similar dreams to mine, and worked their hardest, too...

It saddened me to see the countries where women are not allowed to do for themselves. Some places we went, a tour guide would examine the women on the tour before we got on the shuttle bus, to make sure that all our skin was covered and sometimes our hair. It made me appreciate all over again the fact that my existence proved that not just women have to change their minds but men must change theirs, too, to make cultural revolution possible. I represented a different way for a woman to be and a different way for women to be treated, especially on my business trips. In some ways the financial industry is the largest export America has sent into the world, and although that means exporting its flaws it also means spreading good and useful traits, such as greater equality for women.

I remember a friend of mine, an Asian woman working in the investment advisory business in the 1980s, who was going to open up a China mutual fund. At the time, Asians were very negative about doing anything with women. Anything female was as taboo as going to the bathroom at my parents' card parties. If a man even spoke to a woman, that degraded him. Well, Mrs. Chen went to China to find companies to buy shares for her mutual fund. At one of her first meetings there, she stood at the head of the boardroom table but all the male attendees simply continued talking to each other. None of them would even look at her.

She crawled under the table.

The men leaned down to look at her. One of them asked, "Mrs. Chen, what are you doing under there?"

"Well," she said, "now I have your attention." And she crawled out from under the table and conducted the meeting. She had to get the whole group's attention so that none of the men as individuals would feel inferior for speaking to her.

Every little instance like that one, every time a small, unsung ambassador from America just trying to make a living knocked down a door of bias and misperception, that improved the world. Could a story like that still happen in any country of the world? Well, maybe a few of them.

Indonesia, I think, is emblematic of what not to do as a country. I went there on business once and I was horrified to see these grand facades of beautiful bank offices – with separate entrances for women and with sewers and beggars in the back alleys right behind the banks. That is what it means for a society to be too classist. Everyone should have the ability and opportunity to do for themselves, to keep moving, to pick up their boots and get going.

Personally I think the most important thing to do is to educate the children. Teach children all over the world and the world will do well.

* * *

I kept up with researching the market in between our trips (and with newspapers over every kind of breakfast in every country we traveled to). It wasn't long before the market took another swing – some people call it an adjustment, some people call it a bust. The dot-com businesses went through their sink-or-swim crisis in the year 2000, and a lot of them sank.

Again, if you knew the market, you could have guessed something like that was coming. There had been such euphoria in the late 1990s about this entire new Internet industry. There's nothing wrong with excitement, except when people start to lose their heads. When they feel good, they feel like they just can't lose, so they gamble. They're convinced, how could they be anything but winners! So a lot of people started looking for speculative deals, and well, I've talked about them. All those people found what they wanted: brokers with low morals who were willing and eager to sell risky stocks. And the bill always comes due. Always. For this industry it just happened to come in 2000.

What did I do when the bubble burst? "Buy, buy, BUY!" But only because I had kept up with my research and I knew *what* to buy. That is so important.

Incidentally, FINRA came looking for me – the Financial Industry Regulatory Authority. They used to be the NASD, the organization that had licensed, audited, and supervised my two brokerage firms. Now they wanted me to be an arbitrator for them. I could see how I'd be a sensible choice but

I wasn't interested. Larry, however, was. I love how Larry is so interested in helping the world to run well – he actually looks forward to serving jury duty. How many people are there like that?

Since Larry had been a general principal for Yaeger Capital Markets, he was qualified to arbitrate for FINRA, so he sent in his application and they approved it. He's still arbitrating for FINRA today and they have more work than ever for him. They are running up against a lot of problems in brokerage firms these days, kinds of problems we never saw in my day. For example, firms pay enormous amounts of money to hire brokers and they expect to be repaid by the brokers' efforts. Then the brokers leave and the firms wail, "You owe us!" They sue the brokers and the brokers counter-sue. And that's just the simplest kind of problem FINRA is seeing. In the arbitrations Larry usually finds that both parties are at fault, the brokers and the brokerage firms. The firms are too lax and the brokers are too greedy.

Greed is making everybody crazy, it really is. Sometimes it seems like greed is the mainstay of the business now. We can, and should, regulate the market to minimize the damage. But how do you change people's characters, so that they are less greedy and more steady, more responsible? Maybe we need to teach people that there is a future worth planning for.

Then and Now
Michelle Morton speaks about Norma[8]

Norma was especially unique in the woman- and minority-(w/m) owned side of the financial industry because she saw herself as an investment professional first and a woman second. That was a revolutionary idea twenty years ago and still is today. It is still all too easy to be a w/m-owned business and pitch your firm on that basis alone. Many companies on the client side are just looking to check off the box: "Yes, I do business with a w/m-owned firm." They view it as corporate welfare and they'll take anyone. Many w/m-owned businesses are happy to be treated this way – whatever brings in the money is fine.

Norma didn't settle for that, even when she could have.

The affirmative action programs were very important, but they made one unfortunate mistake. They didn't define what makes a firm "qualified." They didn't establish a growth curve of eligibility, which would have taught firms how to provide the highest level of service, and given them something to aspire to. Therefore, these important set-aside programs simply became handouts.

Norma could have had an easy ride, if she had taken advantage of all the clients who just wanted to check off their boxes. Instead, she insisted that Yaeger Capital Markets *would* be qualified according to the strictest standards – she *would* provide the highest level of service – and that's how she pitched her brokerage firm to every institution she contacted. A client could check off a box if they wanted to, but that wasn't the overriding reason to work with her.

The choice she made was admirable, and the industry would benefit greatly if more people followed her lead.

---

8   In a telephone interview with Clare Kent, May 2012

CHAPTER TWELVE
A Traveler at Heart

PORTOFINO, ITALY: a little curve in the coast with a couple dozen villas, all painted in reds and pinks and golds, the colors of chiffon in a dancer's skirt. An olive green hill rises behind them, the deep blue-green Mediterranean spreads out before them, with sunshine and cloudscapes far above... it is one of the most magical corners of the world. And I can never go back there.

Larry had planned a whole month for us in Europe: meeting friends in Rome, driving through the gorgeous Italian countryside, then over the Dolamites into Germany just in time for Oktoberfest. We were also planning to drive to the hospital in Germany where Larry had been stationed as an Army doctor during the Cuban Missile Crisis, when the Armed Forces in Europe had been preparing for an all-out war with the U.S.S.R.

Our stay in Portofino came early in the trip, and Larry had made reservations at the Hotel Splendido, a world-famous hotspot in that lovely town. I was showering, getting ready for dinner, when I heard Larry say, "I don't believe it. I don't believe it, I don't believe it. Norma?"

I got out of the shower and came into the bedroom where Larry had the TV on. The broadcast was saying that two towers of New York were gone.

At first Larry had thought it was just a program. Then he realized it was the news. We sat on the bed and watched the footage of the planes flying into the buildings, those square-shouldered Twins who were first drawn on an architect's desk just as I was starting my career a few blocks away – the towers that had seemed to guard New York City when I moved to California. They were down. They were gone.

I felt so ill. We canceled dinner. After a few hours we couldn't sit in our room anymore, so we went down to the hotel coffeeshop and watched the TV there. The Italians and tourists gave us such heartfelt condolences... We just sat, for a long time, crying for the loss of all those people.

Then, in our hotel room, we started making phone calls. By that time the phone lines in New York had calmed down a little bit and we could get through to our family. My sister-in-law's nephew had worked in one of the towers, had he made it, was he OK? He was. He had happened to be on the bottom floor so he had been able to run out. A friend of our family, was he all right? Yes. He hadn't gone into work on time so he hadn't been there. A lot of people were fortunate to be late that morning. This was the one time that a bad habit saved lives.

But Cantor Fitzgerald – no one was fortunate there. Cantor Fitzgerald was a big bond house with their headquarters up at the top of the north tower. I had spoken to many traders at that firm, done business with them, had pleasant phone calls with them. They were all dead. Six hundred and fifty-eight employees in one small minute of one terrible day.

It was so horrifying.

The whole country went into mourning. How do you teach people that there is a future worth planning for, with that gruesome rubble smoking at the tip of Manhattan – and really, still smoking today, in the hearts of everyone who was at all close to the people in the buildings and even just the buildings themselves. What do you do? What do you *do*...

Well, you live your life – or else the terrorists win. You live your life as you did before, except that you spend much more time on the parts of your life that are good and important.

There were people who blamed America's foreign policies for provoking such hatred, and some of that blame fell on the stock market and all of the financial industry surrounding it. But following September 11th, 2001, I watched the stock market as if it was my child. I wanted the market to recover and thrive, because people make the market. If people would keep investing for a future, then we would have a future.

Unfortunately, as the past decade has shown, the trend toward short-term investing, with too much money and far too fast, has continued. The future that came down in 2008 brought a four-year recession so brutal it was nearly a depression, and many experts agree that it may not be over yet.

It didn't have to be this way. I know that there are other ways to run and regulate a financial industry, so that everyone can thrive, not just a few big firms and a very small, very greedy slice of the population. I didn't agree with the approaches that the Occupy Wall Street movement used, but I empathized with their message: the financial industry must change, for the betterment of all of us, not just a few.

Maybe this doesn't sound possible to you?

Well, I have made a career out of selling intangibles and I say, it *is* possible. We just need the willpower and fortitude to make it happen. And we need to care about the people who make the market, as well as all the people whose lives are affected by it.

As I wait and watch and hope now, along with everyone else, to see how the future of America unfolds, I am so happy and excited to watch the future of my family develop, too. My family makes it easier to hope on the grand scale. Our children continue to be wonderful parents with successful careers – I know that balance is never easy but they really have a knack. I'm so proud of them.

Stephen, and Nicole too... are never very far from my thoughts and my heart.

And there is this impressive new generation just starting to find their place in the world – the grandchildren! Watching them grow up is as exciting as any trip I have taken. The youngest grandchild, Seth, wants to be a mechanical engineer, which is a truly challenging career, almost an art. He is very, very good at it – good with his hands, and math and science are his best subjects so he is in the right place.

Naomi is taking after her uncle Victor; she's very interested in psychology and wants to do something in that field. Over the past few months she's been waiting to hear from colleges in the UC system about her applications. She'd already been accepted at a few of them but we just heard that the one she wanted most, UC Santa Barbara, has accepted her! She is so excited to go there in the fall.

Callie is a fantastic volleyball player at Amherst College, playing the setter position. She also just took a semester abroad in Denmark, where she is doing research on global warming. She is helping to plan for all our futures and that is a noble cause.

Stacy joined the Peace Corps and she's in Malawi now, working in a clinic, teaching, and writing a blog. She's a wonderful writer – she has the gift – but it's the work in the clinic that is most rewarding to her. She didn't know what she wanted to do after college but now she has an idea: she's thinking of going to graduate school to become a Nurse Practitioner, which would allow her to make diagnoses, write prescriptions, and provide healthcare without consulting a doctor. On that path, she could help make up for the shortage of doctors in this country. I am so impressed with her and I look forward to seeing her grow into her dreams.

David is fluent in Spanish and has just finished his Fulbright fellowship in Mexico City, where he worked for Ashoka, a nonprofit that finances young companies which have a product or service that will benefit the public in some way. He was in charge of reviewing proposals there. When they had a recent opening in their main office in Washington, D.C., he applied and was accepted. He's doing extremely well and has been speaking on their behalf at conferences all over South America.

Larry and I are so proud of all of them and of their parents. It is truly wonderful to look around a table on any given holiday and see such great people in our family.

But they aren't the only ones who are traveling the world and doing amazing things. Larry and I are much older now, but we have never stopped looking for the next adventure. Always keep moving! And not just at the gym! (Although we are careful to do plenty of that, too. Jack LaLanne, I have not forgotten all those good habits you taught me fifty years ago.)

We have been just about every place in the world but Larry did find one place he hasn't seen. This year, our adventure is to travel on a Silversea cruise ship to the North Polar Ice Cap. Not too many non-scientists have done that so we are pioneering again! I have no idea what to expect. Will it be similar to Antarctica? Will it be completely different? As the date approaches for our flight from L.A. to Iceland, where we'll board the cruise ship, I know the anticipation will grow every day for me until I step foot on the plane. Maybe I will even dance a few steps through our living room....

EPILOGUE

I WAS LUCKY to be at the forefront of a major cultural revolution in America, and it has been the great joy and exhilaration of my life to help that revolution happen. I want to tell people about my experience with it so that you have an idea of how to be a revolutionary. Not the flashy, poster child kind of revolutionary, but an ordinary person, feet on the ground, getting a job done – a job that everyone thought was impossible.

Fifty years ago, a woman couldn't have her own bank account or investment account. Now women are CEOs of Fortune 500 companies. Women are involved in every facet of the investment industry – trading, analysis, brokerage firms – and they are on TV and radio and in every aspect of our society (except a few throwback exclusive golf clubs). This level of involvement for women really was considered impossible, but some very special men and women made it possible and made it happen. (Earl Rubin was truly very special.)

We need to keep having cultural revolutions. It's important that no one be handicapped for who they are.

Everyone should be able to pursue what they are capable of doing. There is always the temptation to give up, or to not even try in the first place. But if you're not happy with what you've got, you have to do something about it.

Never let anyone tell you, "You can't do that." Always ask, why? Or, why not? Change the situation so that they say, "Oh you can do that." Or better yet, "Wow, you just did that."

Never take "no" for an answer. If you can't get something done one way, then get it done another way. There is always another way.

If you almost go over a waterfall, get back in the raft and go find the next river. Every time I failed, it made me stronger, more resilient, and ultimately more successful.

If you ever start to feel overwhelmed by reality, just think of how much has changed over the last fifty years. The world can – and probably will – change that much again in the next fifty years. Commit to being part of that change, so that you can help create the world you want to live in.

Make sure you vote, and vote carefully. Pay as much attention to Congressional elections as the Presidential elections – maybe more. Specifically vote for candidates who will support the necessary regulations on the financial industry, or else 2008 is going to happen over and over again. JP Morgan Chase's recent loss of billions of dollars proves that. People don't know how to regulate themselves. Give them a finger and they will take an arm! The government must step in and take that responsibility.

Remember as you vote that government is for the people. It exists so that we can help people who need help. I don't mean helping them by just putting checks in their hands, but by giving them jobs. If there aren't enough jobs available, the government must become an employer, and people must empower the government to do that.

Remember also that our country allows us the right to object, and we are so lucky to have that. We don't live in a dictatorship. It is a wonderful thing that the free world is being exposed all over the globe so that more countries are insisting on and fighting to have democracies. So use your basic rights. Help others to see why those rights are worth fighting for.

And most of all, I encourage you to *always keep moving*, no matter what. That was the secret of my life, and I think it can be the secret of yours, too.

Acknowledgements

The Polar Ice Cap isn't my only adventure right now – there was also the adventure of writing this book, and the ongoing adventure of other people reading it!

My very special thanks to Bettye McCartt-Bogner, who helped to get this book moving by arranging for an introduction to Jeff Rovin. Jeff brought Clare Kent onto the project and was our reliable advisor throughout. It has been wonderful to work with Clare over the past year.

Special thanks to Clare Kent whose dedication to this project and writing skill helped bring my story to life. Without her help this book may not have become a reality.

A big thank you to Norman Bogner, too, an author and dear friend who encouraged me to write the book.

My further heartfelt appreciation to:

Michelle Morton – I love her! She carries my torch.

David Mahler, my lawyer and friend, who helped to keep me out of trouble.

Loretta Sanchez – I have such admiration for her.

Shirley Young – she really came through for me.

Earl and Irma Rubin, my friends and my mentors.

Joe Jackson – where would I be without you?

My daughter-in-law, Susan, who read the book and provided much needed, valuable feedback.

My darling children: Victor, Stephen, Sheri, Elysa, and Tod, and their families. Stephen – I wish you were here.

My mom and dad, Regina and Sam Hason. My siblings: Harvey, Martin, and Nicole. Harvey – without you, I wouldn't have survived. And Nicole – my friend and my partner, I miss you every day.

And of course, my husband and soulmate, who read every chapter of this book multiple times, remembered things I forgot, and relived my memories with me. Thank you for always arranging new, wonderful adventures so that we're not just living on our memories! Larry, you were the strong man behind the strong woman; I could not have done all of this without your support and encouragement.